GUINNESS WORLD RECORDS

WILD THINGS

CONTENTS

DINOLOGY

CONSERVATION CLUB

DANGER ZONE

ZOOTOPIA

ON THE MAP

Editor
Ben Hollingum

Head of Publishing & Book Production
Jane Boatfield

VP Publishing
Jenny Heller

Senior Information & Research Manager
Carim Valerio

Head of Pictures & Design
Michael Whitty

Picture Editor
Fran Morales

Picture Researcher
Saffron Fradley

Senior Editor
Adam Millward

Layout Editor
Diane Pengelly

Editor-in-Chief
Craig Glenday

Senior Managing Editor
Stephen Fall

Gaming Editor
Mike Plant

Talent Researcher
Jenny Langridge

Fact-checking / Proofreading
Karl Shuker, Matthew White

Designer
Billy Waqar

Assistant Designer
Gareth Butterworth

Cover Development
Billy Waqar

Original Illustrations
Olga and Dmytro Bosnak

Augmented-reality Development
AugmentifyIt®: PeaPodicity

Production Director
Patricia Magill

Production Coordinator
Thomas McCurdy

Production Consultants
Roger Hawkins, Tobias Wrona

Reprographics
Res Kahraman at Born Group

Indexer
Marie Lorimer

Printing & Binding
MOHN Media Mohndruck GmbH, Gütersloh, Germany

British Library Cataloguing-in-publication data: a catalogue record for this book is available from the British Library

UK: 978-1-912286-48-5

Records are made to be broken – indeed, it is one of the key criteria for a record category – so if you find a record that you think you can beat, tell us about it by making a record claim. Always contact us before making a record attempt.

Check www.guinnessworldrecords.com regularly for record-breaking news, plus video footage of record attempts. You can also join and interact with the Guinness World Records online community.

Sustainability
The paper used for this edition is manufactured by UPM Plattling, Germany. The production site has forest certification and its operations have both ISO14001 environmental management system and EMAS certification to ensure sustainable production.

UPM Papers are true Biofore products, produced from renewable and recyclable materials.

Guinness World Records Limited has a very thorough accreditation system for records verification. However, while every effort is made to ensure accuracy, Guinness World Records Limited cannot be held responsible for any errors contained in this work. Feedback from our readers on any point of accuracy is always welcomed.

Guinness World Records Limited uses both metric and imperial units. The unit used when the record was originally measured is given first, followed by a converted figure in parentheses. The sole exceptions are for some scientific data where metric units only are universally accepted, and for some sports data. Where a specific date is given, the exchange rate is calculated according to the currency values that were in operation at the time. Where only a year date is given, the exchange rate is calculated from 31 Dec of that year. "One billion" is taken to mean one thousand million.

Appropriate advice should always be taken when attempting to break or set records. Participants undertake records entirely at their own risk. Guinness World Records Limited has complete discretion over whether or not to include any particular record attempts in any of its publications. Being a Guinness World Records record holder does not guarantee you a place in any Guinness World Records publication.

OFFICIALLY AMAZING

CORPORATE OFFICE
Global President: Alistair Richards

Professional Services
Chief Financial Officer: Alison Ozanne
Financial Director: Andrew Wood
Accounts Receivable Manager: Lisa Gibbs
Management Accountants: Jess Blake, Jaimie-Lee Emrith, Moronike Akinyele
Assistant Accountant: Yusuf Gafar
Accounts Payable Clerk: Nhan Nguyen
Accounts Receivable Clerk: Jusna Begum
Senior Finance Analyst: Elizabeth Bishop
Finance Analyst: Tobi Amusan

General Counsel: Raymond Marshall
Senior Legal Counsel: Catherine Loughran
Legal Counsel: Kaori Minami
Legal Counsel, China: Paul Nightingale
Trainee Solicitor: Michelle Phua

Global HR Director: Farrella Ryan-Coker
HR Officer: Monika Tilani
Office Manager: Jackie Angus
Learning & Development Manager: Alexandra Popistan

IT Director: Rob Howe
IT Manager: James Edwards
Developer: Cenk Selim
Desktop Administrator: Alpha Serrant-Defoe
Analyst / Tester: Céline Bacon

Head of Category Management: Jacqueline Sherlock / Victoria Tweedy
Senior Category Manager: Adam Brown
Category Manager: Sheila Mella
Category Executives: Luke Wakeham, Shane Murphy, Jason Fernandes

Global Brand Strategy
SVP Global Brand Strategy: Samantha Fay
Brand Manager: Juliet Dawson
VP Creative: Paul O'Neill

Global Content & Product
SVP Content & Product: Katie Forde
Director of Global TV Content & Sales: Rob Molloy
Senior TV Content Executive & Production Coordinator: Jonathan Whitton
Head of Digital: Veronica Irons
Senior Content Manager: David Stubbings
Social Media Manager: Dan Thorne
Front-End Developer: Alex Waldu
Director of Video Production: Karen Gilchrist
Digital Video Producer: Matt Musson
Junior Video Producer: Cécile Thai / Joseph O'Neil
Audience Development Manager: Sam Birch-Machin
Head of Global Production Delivery: Alan Pixsley
Marketing Director: Helen Churchill
Senior Product Marketing Manager (Brand & Consumer): Lucy Acfield
B2B Product Marketing Manager (Live Events): Louise Toms
B2B Product Marketing Manager (PR & Advertising): Emily Osborn
Product Marketing Executive: Rachel Swatman
Designer: Rebecca Buchanan Smith
Junior Designer: Edward Dillon

EMEA & APAC
SVP EMEA APAC: Nadine Causey
Head of Publishing Sales: Joel Smith
Sales & Distribution Manager: Caroline Lake
Publishing Rights & Export Sales Manager: Helene Navarre

Publishing Sales Executive: Natalie Audley
Commercial Accounts Services Director: Sam Prosser
Senior Account Manager: Jessica Rae
Business Development Manager: Alan Southgate
Commercial Account Managers: Sadie Smith, Fay Edwards, William Hume-Humphreys, Irina Nohailic
Commercial Account Executive: Andrew Fanning

Country Representative – Business Development Manager, India: Nikhil Shukla
Commercial Executive, India: Rishi Nath

Marketing Director: Chriscilla Philogene
Head of PR: Doug Male
Senior Publicist: Amber-Georgina Gill
Senior PR Manager: Lauren Cochrane
Publicist: Georgia Young
PR Assistant: Jessica Dawes
Head of Marketing: Grace Wholey
Senior Commercial Marketing Managers: Mawa Rodriguez, Saloni Khanna
Marketing Manager: Kye Blackett
Marketing Executive: Tiffany Sinclair
Content Marketing Executive: Imelda Ekpo
Content Executive: Connie Suggitt

Head of Records Management APAC: Ben Backhouse
Head of Records Management Europe: Shantha Chinniah
Senior Records Manager: Mark McKinley
Records Managers: Christopher Lynch, Matilda Hagne, Daniel Kidane
Records Executives: Lewis Blakeman, Tara El Kashef

Senior Event Production Manager: Fiona Gruchy-Craven
Event Production Manager: Danny Hickson

Country Manager, MENA: Talal Omar
Head of RMT, MENA: Samer Khallouf
Records Manager, MENA: Hoda Khachab
Senior Marketing Manager, MENA: Leila Issa
Digital Content Executive: Aya Ali
Senior Account Manager: Khalid Yassine
Commercial Account Managers, MENA: Kamel Yassin, Gavin Dickson

VP Japan: Erika Ogawa
Office Manager: Emiko Yamamoto
Director of Records, Japan: Kaoru Ishikawa
Senior Records Manager: Lala Teranishi
Records Manager: Yoko Furuya
Records Executive: Koma Satoh
Senior PR Manager: Kazami Kamioka
PR Assistant: Mina Haworth
Designer: Momoko Satou
Content Manager (Digital): Masakazu Senda
Senior Production Manager: Reiko Kozutsumi
Senior Marketing Manager: Aya McMillan
Commercial Director: Wing Kulshrestha
Sales Manager & Senior Account Manager: Masamichi Yazaki
Senior Account Manager: Takuro Maruyama
Account Managers: Yumiko Nakagawa, Yumi Oda
Assistant: Mina Haworth

Official Adjudicators: Ahmed Gamal Gabr, Anna Orford, Brian Sobel, Glenn Pollard, Jack Brockbank, Kevin Southam, Lena Kuhlmann, Lorenzo Veltri, Lucia Sinigagliesi, Mariko Koike, Paulina Sapinska, Pete Fairbairn, Pravin Patel, Richard Stenning, Şeyda Subası-Gemici, Sofia Greenacre, Victor Fenes, Joanne Brent, Brittany Dunn, Solvej Malouf, Swapnil Dangarikar, Justin Patterson, Mai McMillan, Rei Iwashita, Fumika Fujibuchi, Lasse Lehmann

AMERICAS
SVP Americas: Peter Harper
VP Commercial Account Services: Keith Green
Head of Commercial Account Services: Nicole Pando
Senior Account Managers: Alex Angert, Mackenzie Berry
Account Executive: David Canela
Junior Account Executive: Michelle Santucci
VP Publishing Sales: Walter Weintz
Publishing Sales Manager: Valerie Esposito
Head of RMT, North America: Hannah Ortman
Senior Records Manager, North America: Michael Furnari
Records Managers, North America: Kaitlin Vesper, Spencer Cammarano
Records Executive, North America: Christine Fernandez
Junior Records Executive, North America: Callie Smith
Marketing Director: Sonja Valenta
Senior Marketing Managers: Kerry Tai, Lauren Festa
Junior Designer: Valentino Ivezaj
Head of PR, Americas: Kristen Ott
PR Manager, North America: Elizabeth Montoya
Digital Coordinator: Kristen Stephenson
PR Coordinator, North America: Rachel Gluck
HR Business Partner: Jennifer Olson
Office Assistant: Vincent Acevedo

Head of Brand Development, West Coast: Kimberly Partrick

Director of Latin America: Carlos Martinez
Senior Records Manager, Latin America: Raquel Assis
Senior Account Manager, Latin America: Ralph Hannah
Records Manager, Latin America: Sarah Casson
Account Managers, Latin America: Giovanni Bruna, Carolina Guanabara
PR Manager, Latin America: Alice Marie Pagán-Sánchez
Marketing Manager, Latin America: Laura Angel

Official Adjudicators, North America: Michael Empric, Philip Robertson, Christina Flounders Conlon, Andrew Glass, Claire Stephens, Mike Marcotte, Casey DeSantis, Kellie Parise
Official Adjudicators, Latin America: Natalia Ramirez Talero, Carlos Tapia Rojas, Camila Borenstain

GREATER CHINA
Global SVP Records & General Manager, Greater China: Marco Frigatti
VP Commercial, Global & Greater China: Blythe Fitzwiliam
Senior Account Managers: Catherine Gao, Jacky Yuan, Chloe Liu
Account Managers: Jing Ran, Elaine Wang, Jin Yu
Head of RMT: Charles Wharton
Head of Event Production: Reggy Lu
Event Production Manager: Fay Jiang
Records Manager: Alicia Zhao
Records Executives: Winnie Zhang, Ted Li
Digital Executive: Echo Zhan
PR Manager: Yvonne Zhang
Marketing Director: Karen Pan
Marketing Managers: Maggie Wang, Vanessa Tao, Tracy Cui
Content Director: Angela Wu
HR & Office Manager: Tina Shi
Office Assistant: Crystal Xu
Official Adjudicators: John Garland, Maggie Luo, Dong Cheng, Peter Yang, Louis Jelinek, Wen Xiong, Iris Hou, Cassie Ren

---

WELCOME!

Record-breaking animals have been my constant companions for the last 20 years, as I've travelled the world filming wildlife. I've had the great privilege of dancing an undersea ballet with sperm whales (the **largest-brained animals**), I've dived in Brazilian swamps with green anacondas (the **heaviest snakes**) and been dwarfed by the tail flukes of blue whales (the **largest animals ever**). I've been stung by the **most venomous jellyfish** and by hundreds of bullet ants, which – as I can personally attest! – have the **most painful insect sting**. I've also spent days tracking cheetahs in Africa… I'm guessing you already know what *their* record is!

I have two battered copies of old *Guinness World Records* animal books on my bookshelves, which after many years are very well thumbed! *Wild Things* will doubtless be just as fascinating – especially as we're learning new things about record-breaking animals all the time.

Just recently, for example, we've discovered that the slow-swimming (and poisonous!) Greenland shark, which lives in the cold depths of the North Atlantic, has the **longest lifespan for a vertebrate**; it may live for 400 years or more! Scientists have also unravelled the mysteries behind the awesome vision of deep-sea stomatopods (which are a bit like big, colourful prawns). They have the **most sophisticated eyes of any animal** – and that includes us! Also, a previously unknown population of 1.5 million Adélie penguins has just been reported, living on – and I promise I'm not making this up – the Antarctic Danger Islands.

This wonderful book is full of eye-popping facts about bugs, birds and beasties large and small, as well as some of the incredible conservation initiatives going on right now. Plus – specially interesting for anyone considering a career working with animals – Q&As with some of the mega-stars in the business,

including Sir David Attenborough (pp.148–49), Jane Goodall (pp.142–43), Bindi and Robert Irwin (pp.150–51; pp.160–61) – and me (pp.124–25)!

Animal record-breakers fascinate and enthral us, which helps us to engage with the wonder of nature, and in turn want to protect and conserve it. They also underline the fact that humans are by no means the best at everything! Believing that we're superior to other species is not just plain wrong, it also makes it easier for some people to justify treating animals badly.

Whether it's the lightning-fast tongue of the chameleon (which accelerates faster than a rocket), the immense strength of the Hercules beetle or the phenomenal speed of a sailfish, all these things serve to remind us that we're just one of many animal record-breakers. We happen to be the animal with the greatest ability to change the world we live in – for better or worse. Let's make it for the better!

Steve

Steve is as happy handling snakes as he is meeting underwater wildlife…

INTERVIEW
STEVE BACKSHALL

Find out why – and how – Steve is trying to change people's perceptions of sharks on pp.124–25!

WILD THINGS

Welcome to *Guinness World Records: Wild Things* – the most *roar*-some records book ever!

Join us on a globe-trotting adventure through the animal kingdom. You'll meet nature's giants and mini-beasts, the fastest and the deadliest species, as well as creatures that are so bizarre that they almost defy belief...

In addition to the furry, scaly and feathered record-breaking stars of the natural world, there are also features focusing on zoos, charities and people that have dedicated their lives to conservation. Discover how you too can do your bit for wildlife, even in your own garden!

GWR's Ally Zing (right) is kitted out and ready to go on a superlative safari – are *you*?

MEET ALLY ZING

Welcome to the latest member of the Guinness World Records team: Ally Zing! You can follow Ally's adventures on our kids website – **www.guinnessworldrecords.com/kids** – and over at our PopJam channel. You might even meet him in person at one of our GWR LIVE! events. It's Ally's job to collect the world's most amazing superlatives, so don't be surprised if he turns up at a record attempt near you. It's time to "Bring the Zing!"

Discover the record-breaking animals on each continent with our "On the Map" features.

A species' key info is highlighted in the animal profile cards.

Extra facts, figures and records appear in these trivia bars!

"Infographics" help to put the largest and the smallest creatures into scale.

DID YOU KNOW?

GWR owes its existence to a "wild thing". In the early 1950s, Sir Hugh Beaver of the Guinness Brewery wanted to find out which was Europe's fastest game bird. This quest led to the publication of the first *GWR* book in 1955.

See record-breaking bugs come to life off the page with our special augmented-reality feature on pp.88–89. Look out for this symbol (left) as you read through the book!

Locator maps pinpoint exactly where an animal lives on the planet.

"All Abouts" focus on a single record-breaking species and include an annotated photo highlighting its unique features.

ALL ABOUT CAPYBARAS

Imagine a cross between a Labrador and a guinea pig and you've pretty much got a capybara: the world's *largest rodent*. Arguably, it's also the *"next charming"*.

FLEXIBLE EARS

SHORT FUR

NOSTRILS

PERISCOPE PEEPERS

WHERE IN THE WORLD?

THE PANTANAL

STUBBY TAIL

DESCENDED FROM GIANTS

35 KM/H

Test your wildlife knowledge with our multiple-choice quiz questions!

PROFILE:
DR KARL SHUKER

As Guinness World Records' long-time animals expert, zoologist Karl played a key role in researching the amazing wildlife records inside *GWR: Wild Things*. To date, he has written 26 books and hundreds of articles covering all aspects of natural history. Karl specializes in rediscovered and unrecognized species, as well as record-breaking animals and the beasts of mythology.

BALLOON ZOO

PROFILE: GUIDO VERHOEF

Meet the people behind the records in the "Profile" boxes.

DINOLOGY

Animals have been breaking records for millennia... In our special prehistoric-themed chapter, venture back to the time of the dinosaurs, as we unearth the biggest and baddest reptiles ever to roam our planet.

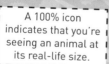

A 100% icon indicates that you're seeing an animal at its real-life size.

BIG PICTURE

100%

TINY TABBY

60 g

Get to know the biggest stars of the wildlife world with our Q&As.

T. REX

INTERVIEW JANE GOODALL

| 58 | 105 | 52 km² | 200+ | 1,500 m |

SAUROPOSEIDON

Quick stats and cool facts offer bonus nuggets of trivia.

How would we have sized up to superlative dinosaurs?!

GRUBBY FINGERS

Madagascar's toothy, big-eared aye-aye may look like a rodent, but it is, in fact, the **largest nocturnal primate**. Males average 65 cm (2 ft 1 in) long, slightly more than half of which is bushy tail. They find food by "percussive foraging": tapping on trees to locate larvae, gnawing holes in the wood with their ever-growing front teeth, and using their extra-long, narrow middle fingers to hook out the grubs... Is that dinner by lucky dip?

ODD BODS

BOOTY AND THE BEASTS

Not just for sitting on, animal backsides have evolved to be multifunctional tools, defensive weaponry, buoyancy aids – and even romantic enticements...

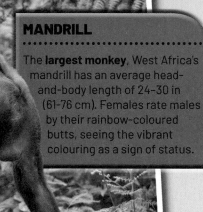

MANDRILL

The **largest monkey**, West Africa's mandrill has an average head-and-body length of 24–30 in (61-76 cm). Females rate males by their rainbow-coloured butts, seeing the vibrant colouring as a sign of status.

DID YOU KNOW?

Scientists have created a fart database. It's not just hot air: animal toots are a serious business, believed to be affecting climate change. Plus, what better way to engage future scientists than with the whiff of a whoopee?

MANATEE

Sirenians (aka sea cows) are herbivorous marine mammals that can eat up to 15% of their own weight a day. All that veg generates a lot of digestive gas – which manatees ingeniously use as a flotation device. They hold in the potential parp to rise in the water – and let rip to sink!

The **longest dive for a sirenian** is 24 min, recorded for a West Indian manatee. That must have been one epic bum burp!

Ooooh that's a relief... GOING DOWN!

REAR-GUARD ACTION

The male twelve-wired bird-of-paradise uses the long black filaments bent over his tush to brush a female's face during courtship. How... cute?

Because sloths leave their trees to poop only once every 5–7 days, they can dump about 20% of their body weight in one go!

Some termites give off methane – a greenhouse gas – when digesting their food. Scientists estimate that termites could produce as much as 150 million tonnes (165 million US tons) of gas a year!

Excuse me!

All together, guys: don't break rank – break wind!

HERRING SHOAL

Atlantic and Pacific herring produce high-frequency sounds at night by releasing air from their backsides. Herring have excellent hearing, so scientists think that the fish use these anal audios to track each other's position. This could help them to form protective shoals when it's dark.

OMG!

Almost 75% of the air a Fitzroy River turtle breathes is sucked in via its butt!

TRAPDOOR SPIDER

This arachnid uses its hard disc of a backside like a manhole cover to seal its burrow. This both disguises the threat to passing prey and protects the spider from potentially deadly wasp stings.

HAWK MOTH CATERPILLAR

Under threat, a hawk moth caterpillar turns itself over to reveal its belly and swells its back end into the shape of a serpent's head. Two black markings acting as the "snake's" eyes complete the genius disguise.

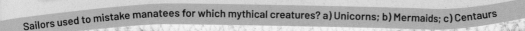
Sailors used to mistake manatees for which mythical creatures? a) Unicorns; b) Mermaids; c) Centaurs

FANG-TASTIC!

This toothy team know gnashers can be used for much more than munching food. Big teeth make for great tools, whether for fighting, hunting or just showing off...

AFRICAN ELEPHANT

The **largest land mammals** boast the **longest tusks** of any living animal, growing to as long as nine bowling pins in a row! These multipurpose tools are used for offence, defence, digging and lifting. Sadly, they're also why many elephants are killed by poachers each year.

WOOLLY MAMMOTH

The **longest mastodon tusks** ever found were longer than a VW Beetle car! Scientists can use rings inside the supersized incisors of these Ice Age giants to estimate an individual's age.

WALRUS

Both male and female walruses have elongated canines. The ivory tusks are handy for digging up food on the seabed, warding off rivals and hauling their huge bodies on to ice floes.

> If I had a dollar for every time I was called long in the tooth...

BATTLE OF THE BITES: How do these giant gnashers measure up?

WOOLLY MAMMOTH: 5 m (16 ft 4 in)

AFRICAN ELEPHANT: 3.4 m (11 ft 5 in)

NARWHAL: 2 m (6 ft 6 in)

WALRUS: 0.9 m (3 ft 1 in)

HIPPOPOTAMUS: 0.5 m (1 ft 7 in)

BABIRUSA: 0.3 m (11.8 in)

SCALE = 0.5 m (1 ft 7 in)

317

Gnashers in the mouth of the common long-tailed gecko: the **most teeth for a living land animal.**

With the price of dental work these days, it's a good job I went extinct!

BABIRUSA

The upper canines of these wild pigs grow so long that they eventually pierce the top of their snouts – *ouch*! Prehistoric paintings of these bizarre-looking swine dating back more than 35,000 years have been found in caves in their native Indonesia.

NARWHAL

Once mistaken for the horn of the mythical unicorn, this feature is actually a tooth. The purpose of the spike – the **longest whale tooth** – baffled scientists for centuries. However, in 2017, a drone filmed narwhals using the tusk to stun cod, so it seems to be (at the very least) a hunting tool.

HIPPOPOTAMUS

Open wide... At 150°, hippos boast the **widest gape for a mammal.** They need such a massive maw to fit their 0.5-m-long (1-ft 7-in) chompers!

At least with one tooth, I don't have to floss!

How many nerve endings are inside a narwhal's super-sensitive tusk? a) 1; b) 300; c) 10 million

ODD BODS

BIG PICTURE

PSYCHEDELIC SEA SLUGS

Bottom-dwelling, jelly-bodied nudibranchs – "naked branches" – come in an array of awesome shapes and colours. Many are toxic to other marine creatures, their vivid colouring serving as a hi-vis warning to potential predators that they really don't make for good snacks...

Found in tropical and temperate seas, as well as Antarctica, they're most common in the shallows, but some dwell as much as 2,500 m (8,200 ft) down.

Pokémon-like blue dragons stand out from the sea-slug crowd in more ways than one. More free-floaters than bottom-grazers, they feed on venomous Portuguese men o' war, a close relative of jellyfish. They absorb their prey's powerful stinging cells and store them to use later against their own enemies.

OMG!

Sea slugs probably see only light and dark, so their brilliant colours are wasted on each other!

IT'S ALL RELATIVE!

The black sea hare, the **largest sea slug**, has been known to grow to 99 cm (3 ft 2 in) and weigh as much as a five-year-old child! Its name comes from its flappy "bunny-ear" tentacles, which are known as "rhinophores".

Nudibranchs do most of their navigating by... a) Smell; b) Touch; c) Marine map-reading

DID YOU HEAR THAT?

Why, Grandma, what big ears you have! All the better to hear you with, my dear. But as these animals prove, good hearing isn't the only advantage that large lugs provide...

1

Super-keen hearing picks up distant squeaks and chirps that let the caracal know where its next meal is hiding!

3

4

2

HOW LOW CAN YOU GO?

Hertz (Hz)

	0	10	20	30	40	50	60	70	80	90	100
GOLDFISH											
PORPOISE											
DOG											
HUMAN											
PIGEON											

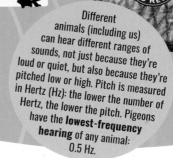

Different animals (including us) can hear different ranges of sounds, not just because they're loud or quiet, but also because they're pitched low or high. Pitch is measured in Hertz (Hz): the lower the number of Hertz, the lower the pitch. Pigeons have the **lowest-frequency hearing** of any animal: 0.5 Hz.

Tuning in to Fox News on longwave...

5

OMG!
These hares were once called "jackass rabbits" because of their donkey-like ears!

6

(1) The caracal, a wild cat from Asia and Africa, relies heavily on its hearing to survive, and uses 20 different muscles to control each of its huge, super-sensitive lugs. The long tufts at the tips are thought to help funnel sounds into the ears.

(2) Big-eared bongos, the **largest forest antelope**, have excellent hearing. This enables them to pick up their many different calls – including grunts, snorts and bleats – in the dense African jungle where they live.

(3) Desert animals such as the long-eared jerboa are often characterized by their oversized ears. With little vegetation in which to hide, small creatures need to hear well – both to catch their dinner and to avoid becoming someone else's!

(4) The spotted bat from Canada, the USA and Mexico has the **longest ears for a bat**. Its translucent pink ears each measure around 5 cm (1.9 in), while its head-and-body length grows only up to 7.7 cm (3 in).

(5) The Sahara desert's fennec fox, with a body just 40 cm (15.7 in) long, plus a bushy tail around half that length, is the **smallest fox species**. Its distinctive bat-like ears radiate body heat to help keep it cool.

(6) When a jackrabbit goes into the shade, the blood vessels in its huge ears widen. Warm blood from the body pumps through the exposed veins, and all the animal's excess heat is lost into the cooler surrounding air. This conserves water, too, as the jackrabbit has no need to pant.

Which type of animal can hear the highest-pitched sounds? a) A fox; b) A moth; c) An eagle

ALL ABOUT NAKED MOLE RATS

Squeamish about rats? Wait till you see a naked mole rat! But don't let their looks scare you away – these record-breaking rodents could one day help us live longer...

Animals don't come much weirder than the naked mole rat, which technically isn't naked, a mole or a rat! These African rodents live in colonies of 100–300 individuals and spend almost their entire lives underground. They're as odd on the inside as they are outside!

Desert mole rats boast several natural superpowers. For one thing, they can survive more than 20 min without oxygen. They're also able to withstand certain types of pain, defy many effects of ageing and are generally immune to cancer; no wonder why these animals are being closely studied by scientists! All this helps to explain why they're the **longest-lived rodents**, living up to 28 years.

EYES
It was long thought that naked mole rats were blind. A 2010 study, however, proved that not only can they detect light, but they also have limited colour vision. They can see blue and green-yellow light.

WHISKERS
Despite their name, naked mole rats aren't totally hairless. Whiskers on the face and fine hairs across the body serve as finely tuned touch sensors.

NAKED MOLE RAT

SCIENTIFIC NAME:	*Heterocephalus glaber*
TYPE:	Mammal
LENGTH:	8–10 cm (3.1–3.9 in)
WEIGHT:	30–80 g (1–2.8 oz)
DIET:	Herbivore, e.g., roots, tubers
LIFESPAN:	Up to 28 years
RANGE:	Eastern Africa

BUCK TEETH
Two long incisors, which move independently, make for useful tools. They can chew through tough plant fibres, attack predators such as snakes and excavate earth when digging.

MOLE RAT VOCATIONS

A mole rat colony is ruled over by the queen. She's responsible for giving birth to all the babies.

A slightly bulkier body makes soldiers well suited to protecting the nest. They do this by standing on top of one another and bearing their teeth!

Most mole rats belong to the worker class. They excavate burrows, collect food and look after the queen's young.

A BUG'S LIFE

Animals such as ants and bees that live and work together, performing jobs as part of a community, are called "eusocial". Naked mole rats are the **most eusocial mammals**. Just like bees, they live in a structured society, with a single breeding female (the "queen"). The others are tasked with building, gathering food and defence (see "Mole rat vocations" above).

4 KM
Mole rats' subterranean homes can include 4 km (2.4 mi) of tunnels, across an area bigger than a football pitch!

WHERE IN THE WORLD?

SUB-SAHARAN AFRICA

Naked mole rats are part of a wider family of burrowing rodents called "blesmols" – all native to semi-arid regions on the edges of the Sahara desert. Owing to little annual rainfall, on the surface, this region is fairly barren. The plants here store a lot of their energy in large roots and tubers, which make up the bulk of these creatures' diet. The range of naked mole rats specifically covers four countries in eastern Africa: Djibouti, Ethiopia, Kenya and Somalia.

BREATHE EASY

Oxygen is limited in mole rats' subterranean homes, so they have evolved small lungs and blood that absorbs oxygen super-efficiently. Air normally contains about 0.04% carbon dioxide, but they can survive in an atmosphere that's up to 80% carbon dioxide!

ELONGATED BODY

The mole rat's sausage-shaped body is perfectly suited to negotiating tight tunnels. These rodents can run backwards as fast as they can forwards!

What do naked mole rats cover themselves in to help recognize each other? a) Food; b) Saliva; c) Poop

PRICKLY PERSONALITIES

Having spikes and spines can make it hard to move – and even harder to make close friends. But one thing's for sure: they really help to get your point across!

OMG!
Red sea urchins – a relative of purple ones – can live for more than 200 years!

1

2

3

4

The aptly named hedgehog snorts, squeals and grunts like a pig as it roots through hedges looking for worms, eggs, snails and frogs.

Hedgehogs have some natural immunity against snake venom, but can still die if they're attacked by one of the more venomous species.

There was no official word for a baby hedgehog until "hoglet" (or sometimes "hedgehoglet") was adopted in the mid-1990s.

When threatened, a porcupine will run backwards and embed its quills into the predator!

I am so the sharpest dresser in town...

1 Purple sea urchins – like all of their spiky kind – have an unusual mouth made up of five toothed, bony plates. They use this to chomp pieces out of rock to make a "nest", then use their spines to wear away the surface even further.

2 Relatives of the Algerian hedgehog (pictured) were domesticated in the 4th century BCE by the Romans. The spiny mammals were raised mostly for their meat and quills, but some were also kept as the **first pet hedgehogs**.

3 A spiny devil katydid from South America sports not only a fine array of spikes, but also antennae that can be as long as its body! Although this prickly cricket is a master of camouflage, it's not afraid to take on much larger foes.

4 With spines, beaks and temporary pouches, echidnas are among Australia's oddest critters. One rare species of these egg-laying mammals has been named after naturalist Sir David Attenborough (see pp.148–49).

5 Weighing up to 27 kg (59 lb), the North African crested porcupine is the **largest porcupine**. Its name comes from the quills on its head and back, which raise to form a Mohican-like hairdo.

6 Australia's desert-dwelling moloch, or thorny devil, eats only small black ants, giving it the **most restricted lizard diet**. It licks up ant trails with its sticky tongue and can gobble up 1,000 of the piqu-*ant* bugs in a single sitting!

Which is the only mammal, other than the echidna, to lay eggs? a) Platypus; b) Whale; c) Tiger

INTERVIEW
COYOTE PETERSON

Close animal encounters and wild adventures are guaranteed in Coyote's YouTube videos, posted on his record-breaking animal channel, Brave Wilderness.

What first interested you in nature and wildlife?

Growing up in Ohio, I'd spend my time exploring the wild areas behind my home. Forests, creeks, swamps and a hidden lake add up to an endless opportunity for adventure! My number-one animal infatuation was the common snapping turtle [see "No pain, no gain!" opposite].

Who inspires you?

Regarding animals, adventure and film-making, my top three inspirations are Steve Irwin, Bear Grylls and Steven Spielberg.

Is YouTube changing the way people engage with nature?

Oh, yes. There's such creative freedom and it reaches such a wide audience. Via YouTube, we've been able to bring an important message about conservation to a whole new generation of future explorers.

How did your being stung and bitten become such a big part of Brave Wilderness?

Episodes featuring bites and stings have played a big part in the channel's speedy growth, but pain wasn't part of our initial design!

It began with me being quilled by a porcupine – we wanted to show how to remove quills in the right way. From there, it was snapping turtle bites, alligator bites, insect stings and all kinds of craziness. To be honest, the pain part was a bit of a drag. But once the episodes were released and millions of people were watching – and most importantly *learning* about these bizarre creatures – it was worth the agony. "Wow factor" content is gripping, but it's only about 10% of what makes up Brave Wilderness.

Which animal has given you the most painful sting or bite?

The worst bite – actually a two-clawed pinch – was by the giant desert centipede. That sent me to hospital. Its venom attacks your red blood cells, exploding them from the inside out! My arm swelled up to three times its normal size and the

Coyote eyeballs a toothy sockeye salmon. The millions of eggs these fish lay provide food for everything from bears to rainbow trout.

pain was so intense I couldn't sit still. The worst sting came from the bullet ant [see p.74]. The pain made me feel as if my arm had been dipped in lava! And the worst part is there is no anti-venom for either of them – you just have to sit it out.

Are there any animals you'd never contemplate doing a video with?

No – in fact, we're hoping to do big

TAKING *TWO* FOR THE TEAM

According to statistics tracker Social Blade, Brave Wilderness is the **most subscribed YouTube channel dedicated to animals**, with more than 9.7 million subscribers as of 15 Mar 2018. Since the channel opened in 2014, it's had more than 1.6 billion views, which also makes it the **most viewed animal channel on YouTube**. Coyote shares the honours with director Mark Laivins, wildlife biologist Mario Aldecoa, and editors Chris Kost and Ryan Gebrura, as well as many other contributors.

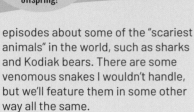

episodes about some of the "scariest animals" in the world, such as sharks and Kodiak bears. There are some venomous snakes I wouldn't handle, but we'll feature them in some other way all the same.

What animals do you most want to feature on your channel?
Oh, just the dream species: the great white shark, Komodo dragon, anaconda, polar bear, Tasmanian devil and bald eagle, to name just a few... Though probably not all of them in the same episode!

A wild ocelot – twice the size of the average house cat – play-fights with Coyote during a night-time adventure in Costa Rica.

Where's the most exotic location you've travelled to?
Costa Rica with its epic rainforests is probably the most exotic, but when it comes to an open expanse of wilderness, Alaska is by far the greatest place I've been.

Has anything ever gone wrong when filming?
Things go wrong all the time! Everything from not managing to catch an animal, to falling off cliffs. There are also funny moments:

I often get pooped or peed on by an animal that I'm handling.

Do you think some animals unfairly get a bad reputation?
Yes! In fact, almost all creepy-crawlies seem to have an unwarranted bad rap. Take spiders, for example. Many people are scared of spiders no matter how big or small, but spiders have no interest in us – plus they eat the pesky insects that drive us crazy, such as flies and mosquitoes. I think if you're afraid of something, it's a good idea to find out about it so that you understand it better – that usually helps.

How does it feel to hold two Guinness World Records titles?
AMAZING! As a kid, I always hoped that one day I would hold a world record... for doing something silly like eating more gummy worms than anyone ever! It's an incredible honour, and one that we as a team hold very dear.

Do you have any animals at home?
We have a dog named Charlie Bear, seven baby snapping turtles (which we're looking forward to releasing this spring) and a sulcata tortoise named Green Bean.

What's the one thing we should be doing to aid wildlife conservation?
It all starts with education. The more you know about a specific animal and its environment, the

better. One of the best ways to do that is to get outside and explore. The world is full of adventure and teeming with fascinating animals, so be brave, stay wild... and we'll see you on our next YouTube adventure!

Better bee brave and bite the bullet – as long as it's not the bullet ant that's biting me...!

ODD BODS

23
Domestic cat and dog tails have at most only half as many bones as long-tailed pangolin tails!

When they feel under threat, pangolins curl up into a ball. The jagged scales act like a suit of armour to put off predators.

IT'S ALL RELATIVE!

The black-bellied scaly anteater shares its central and western Africa territory with the **largest pangolin**. Giant pangolins can reach 2 m (6 ft 6 in) – about the same length as a king-size bed!

My cousin never stops going on about his tail...

THE WALKING PINECONE

The long-tailed pangolin, aka the black-bellied pangolin, has between 46 and 47 vertebrae in its tail: the **most tail bones for a mammal**. Despite this, it's actually the **smallest pangolin**, reaching only 60–80 cm (1 ft 11 in–2 ft 7 in) long – more than half of which can be tail! Pangolins, which are also known as scaly anteaters, owe their pinecone-like appearance to an outer layer of large, overlapping scales. Made of the same stuff as our fingernails – keratin – these scales protect pangolins from predators, as well as the stings of termites and ants.

BIG PICTURE

GUINNESS WORLD RECORDS

STICKING THEIR NECKS OUT

A long neck gives you many ways to get ahead: you can see far above the crowd, reach high for the tastiest food or snatch prey before it has even seen you coming.

GIRAFFE WEEVIL

No guessing how this bug got its name! Native to Madagascar, male giraffe weevils use their amazing necks to fight rivals, while females use theirs (which are much shorter) to help build nests.

OMG!

A giraffe's tongue can stretch up to 50 cm (20 in)!

EASTERN LONG-NECKED TURTLE

Also called the snake-necked turtle, this reptile hangs out in slow-moving water such as ponds and streams in eastern Australia. Its neck grows to around 25 cm (10 in) – almost as long as its shell.

GIRAFFE

Native to Africa's sub-Saharan savannah, the **tallest mammal** can grow to 5.5 m (18 ft) – so could rest its chin on the roof of a double-decker bus! The giraffe has the **longest animal neck**; it accounts for around one-third of its height. This extraordinary feature helps them to keep a lookout and to graze from the treetops.

Relative to body size, *Omeisaurus tianfuensis* was the **longest-necked dinosaur**. Its neck contained 17 bones and was four times longer than its body!

Owls have the **farthest head rotation of any animal**. From facing forwards, these birds can twist their heads 200° in each direction – so that's a total of 400°. What a hoot!

The **longest human neck extension**, achieved by women of the Padaung tribe of Myanmar, is 40 cm (15.7 in). A full set of 25 rings can weigh as much as 10 kg (22 lb).

GERENUK

With elongated limbs and neck, this gangly gazelle lives among woody vegetation in East Africa. The gerenuk – which means "giraffe-necked" in Somali – is the only antelope that can stand on its hind legs. This means it can forage higher in the trees than most of the competition.

ANHINGA

This aquatic bird, with its long, serpentine neck, lives in the warmer parts of the Americas. The anhinga – aka "snakebird" – swims low in the water, often with only its neck and head exposed, so looks like a snake about to strike. It uses its dagger-like bill to spear fish.

FRILLED DRAGON

The frill-necked lizard of Australia likes to blend in to its forest home, but if cornered it does have a trick up its neck... Gaping its mouth triggers a colourful ruff of skin to open up like an umbrella. This usually causes a predator to pause just long enough for the "frilly" to make a quick getaway!

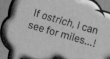

If ostrich, I can see for miles...!

OSTRICH

The **largest bird** (see p.54) also has the **longest neck for a bird**, measuring around 0.9 m (3 ft). Its unique construction lets an ostrich reach the ground without bending its legs and turn its head through 180°.

Which animal has more than three times as many neck bones as you do? a) A swan; b) A giraffe; c) A llama

NORTH AMERICA

North America has everything from snow-capped mountains to scorching-hot deserts. Its animal life is just as varied...

Largest deer
Alaskan moose can measure 2.3 m (7 ft 6 in) tall and weigh as much as a small car. Most of their height comes from their long legs, which help them to walk through deep snow. Moose are not carnivores, but their size and strength mean they are still very dangerous.

Largest canid
The grey wolf, which is found throughout the northern hemisphere, is the **largest canid** (dog-like animal). Grey wolves measure up to 81 cm (2 ft 7 in) at the shoulder and can be as much as 1.6 m (5 ft 2 in) long, excluding the tail. Some of the biggest live in Canada and Alaska, USA.

Smelliest mammal
The striped skunk is famous for its unusual defence mechanism. When threatened, it sprays its foes with a foul-smelling liquid, which puts them right off the idea of eating a skunk (or anything really) for a long time. Skunks can spray this liquid as far as 3 m (10 ft)!

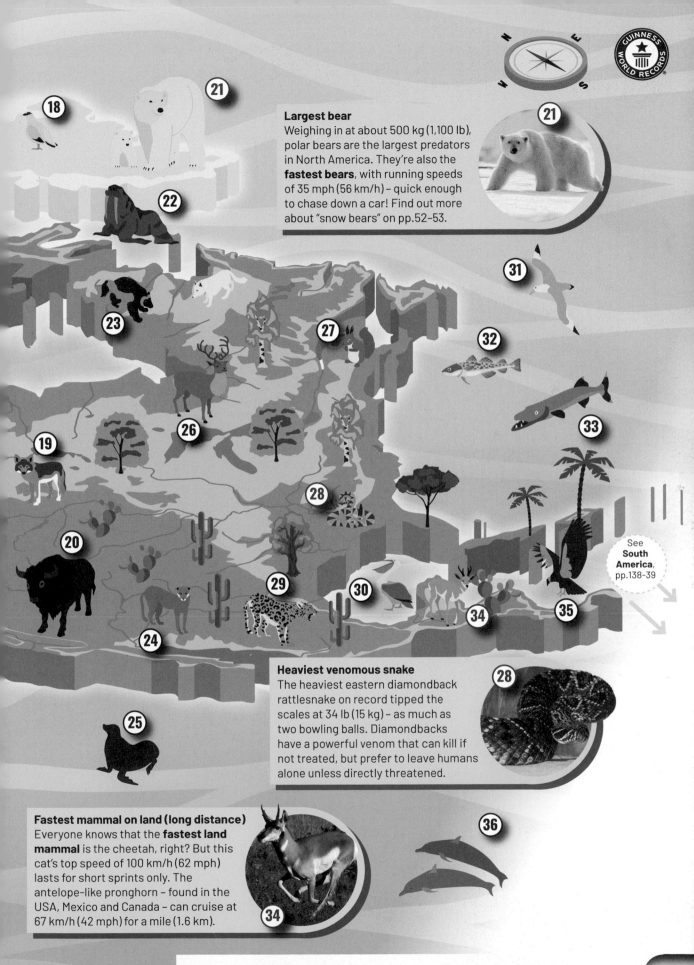

Largest bear
Weighing in at about 500 kg (1,100 lb), polar bears are the largest predators in North America. They're also the **fastest bears**, with running speeds of 35 mph (56 km/h) – quick enough to chase down a car! Find out more about "snow bears" on pp.52–53.

See **South America**, pp.138–39

Heaviest venomous snake
The heaviest eastern diamondback rattlesnake on record tipped the scales at 34 lb (15 kg) – as much as two bowling balls. Diamondbacks have a powerful venom that can kill if not treated, but prefer to leave humans alone unless directly threatened.

Fastest mammal on land (long distance)
Everyone knows that the **fastest land mammal** is the cheetah, right? But this cat's top speed of 100 km/h (62 mph) lasts for short sprints only. The antelope-like pronghorn – found in the USA, Mexico and Canada – can cruise at 67 km/h (42 mph) for a mile (1.6 km).

How many animals can you identify on this map? See pp.186–87 for answers.

FUR THE WIN!

If there were a record for **"cutest animal"**, the sea otter would be a top contender. With approximately 100,000–400,000 hairs on every 1 cm^2 of its body (650,000–2.6 million hairs per sq in), it has the **densest fur** of any mammal. This thick coat helps keep these marine creatures warm in the chilly waters off Russia and North America.

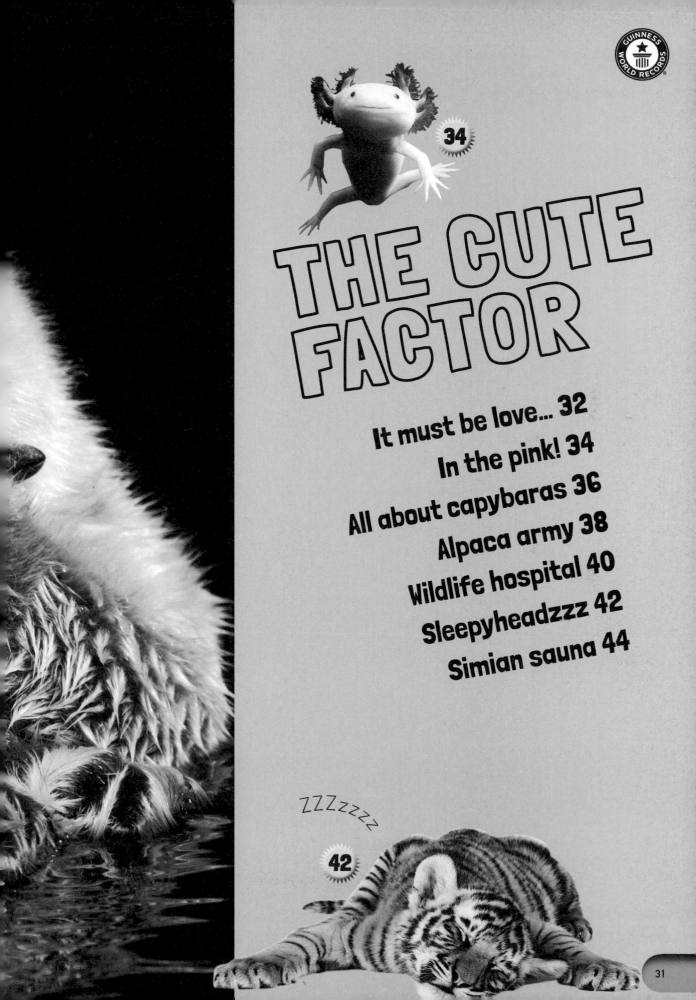

THE CUTE FACTOR

34

zzZZzzz

42

GUINNESS WORLD RECORDS

IT MUST BE LOVE...

True love isn't exclusive to humans... While some animals only meet to produce the next generation, others seek each other out yearly, or even become life-long companions!

HYACINTH MACAW

Native to South America, these blue beauties are the **longest parrots**, measuring up to 1 m (3 ft 3 in). Pairs of the highly sociable birds are faithful to each other for life.

EUROPEAN BEAVER

Beavers – at least in Europe – are monogamous (i.e., stay with one partner). This behaviour lowers the risk of desertion, which is important in species where both sexes care for their offspring. DNA tests reveal that North American beavers, meanwhile, are more fickle!

MUTE SWAN

Until one of them dies, mute swan couples almost always stay together. Widowed swans usually mate again – females sometimes within a few weeks. Males tend to wait until the following autumn or winter to find new love, defending their nests and raising their cygnets in the meantime.

74,000

The number of mute swans that over-winter in the UK, compared to 6,400 resident pairs.

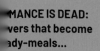

MANCE IS DEAD:
vers that become
ady-meals...

A female octopus, larger and hungrier than her male, may well strangle and eat him after mating.

Love hurts! During mating, the female praying mantis (see pp.82–83) may bite off her partner's head and then devour his corpse.

Black widow spiders often eat the (smaller) males. Oddly, the male sometimes seems to welcome his fate, actively throwing himself into his partner's fangs!

LAYSAN ALBATROSS

These huge birds are not only monogamous, but they also celebrate their bond with a special courtship dance. Wisdom (left), the **oldest breeding sea bird**, seen here with her partner Akeakamai, laid her 42nd egg at the age of 67 in 2017. The pair return each year to Midway Atoll, in Hawaii's Papahānaumokuākea marine park, to nest. Wisdom has probably raised 30–35 chicks, outliving several of her mates.

It gets harder every year to think of baby names...

You read the bed-time story, dear; I'll put the bins out.

SHINGLEBACK SKINK

When he finds a mate, Australia's pinecone lizard – aka stumpy – will stay by her side for weeks before the mating ritual begins. He'll then pair up with the same female every spring for 20 or more years.

AZARA'S NIGHT MONKEY

The **heaviest night monkey**, from South America, weighs about 1.25 kg (2 lb 12 oz). Couples stay faithful to each other, and males share the childcare.

Shingleback skinks are sometimes called "blueys" owing to the colour of their... a) Feet; b) Tails; c) Tongues

IN THE PINK!

There's no missing these candy-floss critters. Hang out with blushing beasties like these and you can leave your rose-tinted glasses behind!

Spider-Man wishes he could pull this look off as well as me!

1

While male Mwanza flat-headed agama lizards are brightly coloured, the females are mainly brown.

3

4

2

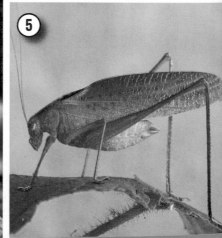

5

BLUES BROTHERS

Up to a million overlapping scales in the blue morpho's wings reflect light to create their colour.

The regal blue tang is part of the "surgeonfish" family, named for their sharp, scalpel-shaped spines. Males use the spines in "sword fights".

The toxin in blue poison-dart frogs' skin can kill, but their bright colour warns predators not to eat them.

(6)

There are six species of flamingo: two native to the Old World and four to the New World (Americas).

(7)

Pink isn't just a colour – it's an attitude!

(1) The Mwanza flat-headed rock agama – aka the Spider-Man agama because of its superhero colours – lives in small groups in eastern Africa. The most vividly coloured male is often the leader.

(2) Mexico's newt-like axolotl can adjust its colour to hide. Odder still, it spends most of its life as a teenager! In 2018, the axolotl's DNA was found to contain 32 billion base pairs: the **largest amphibian genome**.

(3) Genetic tests in 2013 revealed that this neon-pink Australian mollusc wasn't a red triangle slug as first thought, but a new species. This earned the as-yet-unnamed creature the coveted title of **newest slug**.

(4) The rosy maple moth's candy-coloured coat of dense fuzz comes complete with matching legs and antennae. Its bright colours are designed to warn potential predators that it doesn't taste good!

(5) Bush crickets, aka katydids, come in green, tan and yellow... but around one in 500 are bright pink. Their stand-out colour could partly account for their rarity, as it makes them easy for enemies to spot!

(6) Flamingos' pink plumage comes from chemicals in their food. They "filter feed", using their upside-down bills to capture brine shrimp and algae from the silt.

(7) The Amazon's boto – the **largest river dolphin** at 2.6 m (9 ft) long – owes its rosy hue to blood vessels under its skin that help to regulate body temperature.

Which of these is *not* a name for a group of flamingos? a) A flock; b) A flamboyance; c) A flatulence

ALL ABOUT CAPYBARAS

Imagine a cross between a Labrador and a guinea pig and you've pretty much got a capybara: the world's **largest rodent**. Arguably, it's also the **"most charming"** ...

Rodents such as rats and mice often feature among lists of the most scary and reviled animals. So you may ask what on Earth we were thinking putting the **largest rodent** in a chapter all about *cute* critters... But just look at these guys!

About the size of a medium dog, capybaras live in wetland areas of Central and South America. They divide their time between the water, wallowing in mud and grazing on the banks. Their bodies are perfectly adapted for a semi-aquatic lifestyle.

Social animals, they live in families of 10–20 individuals, usually with a ratio of two females to every one male. Living in a group like this has the advantage of having more eyes to look out for potential enemies. If attacked, adults huddle around younger members of the family to protect them.

WHERE IN THE WORLD?

THE PANTANAL

One of the best places to see capybaras is the world's **largest wetland**. Straddling Brazil, Bolivia and Paraguay, the Pantanal covers an area two times larger than Ireland (or roughly the same size as the US state of Illinois). The swamp is home to a wide array of supersized creatures beyond the capybara, including the **largest jaguar subspecies**, the **largest caimans**, and 1-m-long (3-ft 3-in) hyacinth macaws, the **longest parrots**.

STUBBY TAIL
Unlike many rodents, capybaras have only a small, barely visible stump.

CAPYBARA

SCIENTIFIC NAME:	*Hydrochoerus hydrochaeris*
TYPE:	Mammal
LENGTH:	1–1.3 m (3 ft 3 in–4 ft 3 in)
WEIGHT:	Up to 79 kg (174 lb)
DIET:	Herbivore, e.g., grass, aquatic plants, fruit
LIFESPAN:	4–8 years
RANGE:	Central America and South America

WEBBED FEET
Hoof-like nails help with swimming and gripping on to muddy river banks.

CAPYBARA TRIVIA

In the 1500s, these semi-aquatic mammals were classed as "fish". This meant Catholics could eat them on holy days, such as Lent, when traditionally they don't eat meat.

Don't get too close to a capybara: its breath can be pretty whiffy! That's largely because they eat their own poop – a practice called "coprophagy". They do this to get as many nutrients out of their food as they possibly can.

A few people have raised capybaras as pets, even though they're tricky to look after and need lots of space. The gigantic guinea pigs have proven to be highly intelligent and sociable animals. One called JoeJoe (right) is the **most followed capybara on Instagram**, with 119,000 followers!

FLEXIBLE EARS
These press flat against the head when the capybara is swimming.

SHORT FUR
Capybaras' wiry hair dries out quickly – useful when you're constantly in and out of water.

NOSTRILS
Special flaps in the capybara's nose stop water getting in.

PERISCOPE PEEPERS
Eyes are positioned on the top of their heads so they can still look out for danger, even when almost fully submerged.

35 KM/H
As well as being great swimmers, capybaras can run about as fast as a pony on land (21.7 mph)!

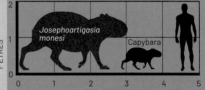

DESCENDED FROM GIANTS

Josephoartigasia monesi

Capybara

If you think the capybara is big, you should see one of its prehistoric ancestors... Though *J. monesi* (above left) looked similar to a capybara, the **largest rodent ever** is genetically more closely related to a fellow South American critter called the pacarana.

LEGS
The limbs are short and stocky – good for swimming – with the rear legs slightly longer than the front ones.

STAYING ALIVE
Although capybaras have size on their side, they are not without their enemies. Big cats, such as jaguars and pumas, are their main predators, but they are also sometimes targeted by anacondas, caimans and opportunistic harpy eagles. Their main defence is to flee into water. They are strong swimmers and can hold their breath for as long as five minutes!

What sound do capybaras make when they want to raise the alarm? a) Squeak; b) Purr; c) Bark

THE CUTE FACTOR

DID YOU KNOW?

To communicate with one another, alpacas have developed a range of humming sounds. These are particularly attuned between a mother and its cria (baby alpaca), with different hums to indicate fear and hunger, among other feelings.

The alpacas weren't the only ones to get smart for the parade. Many of their owners donned traditional Peruvian dress too.

IT'S ALL RELATIVE!

The **smallest species of camel** – and thought to be the wild ancestor of the alpaca – is the vicuña. Living at heady heights of 4,800 m (15,750 ft) in South America's Andes mountains, they stand just 90 cm (2 ft 11 in) at the shoulders.

BIG PICTURE

ALPACA ARMY

A fluffy herd of 460 well-groomed alpacas strutted their stuff on the streets of Macusani, Peru, on 21 Aug 2017, as part of the **largest alpaca parade**. The mountain town is regarded as the country's "alpaca capital", with some 20,000 of these domesticated llama relatives in the region. Alpaca fleece is prized the world over for its warmth and softness – it's far less scratchy than sheep's wool!

Which of these animals is not native to Peru? a) Andean condor; b) Aardvark; c) Spectacled bear

THE CUTE FACTOR

WILDLIFE HOSPITAL

Each year, Tiggywinkles Wildlife Hospital in Buckinghamshire, UK, cares for more than 10,000 animals and deals with over 70,000 calls for help from around the world...

Tiggywinkles vets have to improvise splints and bandages to fit animals of all shapes and sizes, such as this lapwing chick.

The hospital first became known for hedgehogs, and it pioneered their treatment, which explains its name [see "Tiggywinkles in-patients", top right]. But hedgehogs are now just a part of a much bigger story.

These two orphaned otter cubs were found on a stormy night, freezing cold and crying out for their mother. The pair had probably been washed from their "holt" (underground burrow) during heavy rains and flooding. Tiggywinkles swung into action, warming them up and settling them in with their first bottle-feed. The pair were later successfully released back into the wild.

Tawny owlets on the ground aren't necessarily lost or orphaned and are often best left alone. They go through a phase called "branching", when they start exploring beyond their nests.

We really otter stop fur-ever posing for impawsibly cute photos...

365
Days a year that Tiggywinkles is open to care for sick, injured and orphaned wildlife.

Otter orphans need to be looked after for longer than most animals, because in the wild they would stay with their mother for up to a year. Once weaned, Tiggywinkles cubs move into a monitored outdoor enclosure – complete with pools for swimming practice!

Tiggywinkles hospital treats so many hedgehogs that it took its name from *The Tale of Mrs Tiggy-Winkle*, a book by Beatrix Potter about a hedgehog washerwoman.

Aside from hedgehogs, the next most common mammal patients are deer. At least one arrives at the hospital every day!

About 60% of all patients are garden birds such as blue tits. Birds that forage in roadside hedgerows are the most likely to be admitted.

Tiggywinkles takes in about 100 badgers a year – many with bite wounds. After treatment, they're moved to an outdoor pen to reacclimatise. Once they have the vets' all-clear, they are returned to their home range and released.

Adult muntjac deer are difficult to treat, as they have tusks, antlers and pointy hooves... but this tiny orphaned fawn was much less of a "handful"!

You should never try and pick up an injured badger – they have sharp claws and a powerful bite! Call in your local wildlife rescue team.

PROFILE: COLIN STOCKER, Tiggywinkles Hospital Manager

Why did your family set up Tiggywinkles?

My father [Les Stocker], who had a passion for wildlife, realized that there were no facilities in Britain for treating injured wild creatures. Vets were given just half a day's tuition as their "wildlife training"! So he set about teaching himself, and word soon spread.

In 1991, we opened the first Wildlife Teaching Hospital. Since then, thousands of vets, nurses and rehabilitators from around the world have come here to study. We're now also in the process of building a college in Dad's memory.

How many animals have been treated at Tiggywinkles?

It must be well over 300,000 by now. We have roughly 1,500 in-patients on any *one day* in the summer! That's a whole lot of mouths to feed...

Any unusual creatures?

Albino animals are quite unusual – we've seen white otters, foxes, badgers and hedgehogs. Our specialist vets also bring in the occasional "exotic"; the odd leopard keeps us on our toes!

What about unusual rescues?

We were called out once to rescue a badger who had fallen into a drained swimming pool and couldn't climb out. He gave us quite the run-around before my father eventually caught him! Thankfully he was unharmed so could be released safely back home.

We also took on a tiny otter that had fallen into a fast-moving river. A quick-thinking punter [a punt is a flat-bottomed boat pushed along with a pole] paddled after the cub and managed to scoop him out. The otter was brought into our care to join other cubs who were being hand-reared.

Which animals rub themselves with plant poison as a form of defence? a) Ducks; b) Hedgehogs; c) Deer

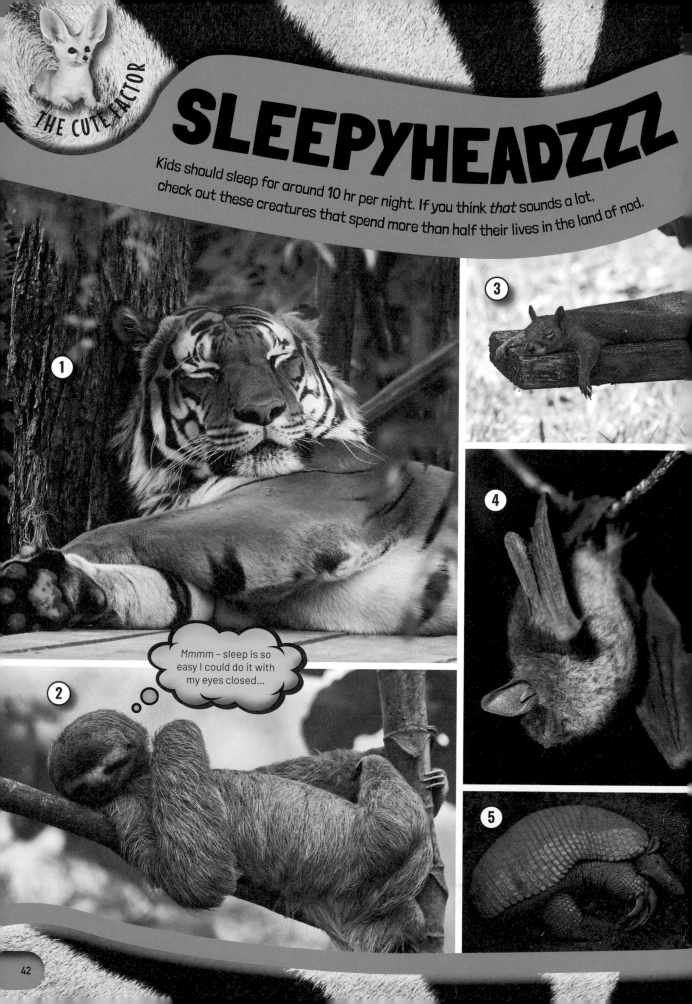

THE CUTE FACTOR

SLEEPYHEADZZZ

Kids should sleep for around 10 hr per night. If you think *that* sounds a lot, check out these creatures that spend more than half their lives in the land of nod.

Mmmm – sleep is so easy I could do it with my eyes closed...

MONTHS ASLEEP

WINTER-TIME SNOOZERS	0	1	2	3	4	5	6	7	8	9	10	11	12
BUMBLEBEE							▪	▪	▪	▪			
BROWN BEAR							▪	▪					
HEDGEHOG						▪	▪						
COMMON POORWILL					▪	▪							
BOX TURTLE				▪	▪								

The thick and dotted bars on the chart indicate a range: e.g., the bee spends between six and nine months dozing, depending on local conditions such as climate.

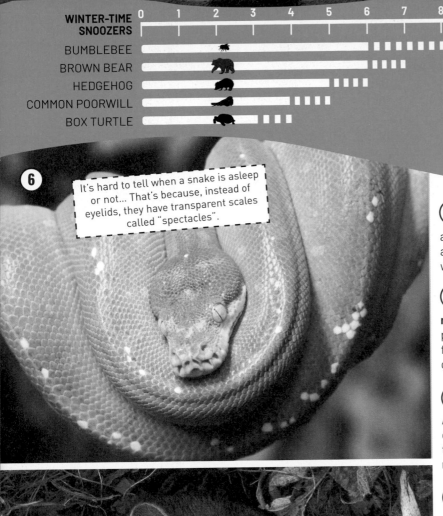

6

It's hard to tell when a snake is asleep or not... That's because, instead of eyelids, they have transparent scales called "spectacles".

1 The **largest wild cats** (see also pp.136–37) spend nearly 16 hr a day cat-napping. Tigers are more alert in the mornings and evenings, when they prefer to hunt.

2 The three-toed sloth of tropical South America – the **slowest mammal** – averages 1.8–2.4 m (6-8 ft) per minute on the ground. To recover from these "exhausting" sprints, it too gets around 16 hr of daily shut-eye.

3 Squirrels clock up nearly 15 hr a day asleep. During hibernation, Arctic ground squirrels take "chilling out" to another level, achieving the **lowest body temperature in a mammal**: a frosty -3°C (26°F)!

4 Little brown bats are zippy, mouse-sized critters about as heavy as a strawberry. They get the **most sleep for a mammal**: as much as 19.9 hr a day! They hunt by night, and hibernate for four to six months.

5 The giant armadillo has the **most teeth for a land mammal** (100) and the **longest claws on a living animal** (20 cm; 7.8 in). But all that chomping and scratching must take its toll as it enjoys 18-hr naps!

6 Green tree pythons spend most of their lives – including some 18 hr asleep per day – elegantly coiled over branches. Pythons are the **longest reptiles**; one reticulated python measured 10 m (32 ft 9 in).

7 North America's eastern chipmunk spends the **longest time inactive at home**. It can remain in its hole, living off a store of nuts, for as long as a year at a time without venturing outside once.

7

Chipmunks spend as much as 15 hr per day in the land of nod!

Which mammal gets the least sleep, clocking as little as two hours per day? a) A hippo; b) An African elephant; c) A kangaroo

BIG PICTURE

SIMIAN SAUNA

Japanese macaques, aka snow monkeys, chill out in a mountainous area of Japan called Jigokudani – "Hell's Valley". Living as far as 36°N, they're the **most northerly primates** (apart from humans), and survive the -15°C (5°F) winters by warming themselves in hot volcanic spring water. Pool temperatures can reach 43°C (109°F), so the monkeys test the water carefully before easing themselves in. They climb out before nightfall, giving themselves time to dry off – otherwise, they would risk freezing to death.

While the grown-ups snooze in the pool, playful youngsters enjoy a snowball fight – much like their human cousins!

IT'S ALL RELATIVE!

The **most southerly primates** (other than humans) are chacma baboons. They live in South Africa's Cape Peninsula at a latitude of 34°S. Also the **largest baboons**, they grow to a maximum weight of 40 kg (88 lb).

DID YOU KNOW?

A new food fad quickly spread after one snow monkey tried rinsing her potato in the river, rather than just brushing it clean. She then tried dipping it in salty ocean water between bites for a light seasoning – and soon the whole troop followed her lead!

Snow monkeys forage fruits and berries then store them for later in their... a) Caves; b) Cheeks; c) Handbags

AFRICA

Teeming with fish, reptiles, birds and mammals, the world's second-largest continent arguably boasts the lion's share of animal records...

Fastest bird on land
Unable to fly, an ostrich uses its powerful legs to attain speeds of up to 45 mph (72 km/h) – nearly twice as fast as the world's **fastest man**, Usain Bolt! At 9 ft (2.7 m) tall, it's also the **largest living bird**; it would reach about halfway up an adult giraffe (see opposite).

See **Asia**, pp.90-91

Most social big cats
Whereas other big cats prefer to live alone, lions hang out in "prides". Most prides have five or six lionesses, a few cubs and one or two adult males, but some have as many as 30 individuals. A lone lion or lioness is known as a "nomad".

Tallest mammal
At up to 5.5 m (18 ft) tall, a giraffe stands more than three times the height of a typical man. Giraffes are born tall – a newborn is already about as long as its mother's legs. It grows to out-reach competitors for its favourite snack of acacia leaves.

Greatest land migration
Between 1 and 2 million wildebeest make the round trip each year from the Serengeti plains of Tanzania to Kenya, across the Mara River. Many other animals – such as zebras (and their hungry predators!) – join them in their never-ending search for pasture.

Largest terrestrial mammal
Weighing about the same as 11 polar bears, the African elephant eats monster quantities of vegetation to maintain its 4,000–7,000-kg (8,800–15,400-lb) mass. Even a baby – at 1 m (3 ft 3 in) long – is about as heavy as three Dalmatian dogs!

Largest tail
At up to 17 ft 4 in (5.2 m) across, a humpback whale's tail is as wide as a giraffe is tall. The whale uses it not only to power the **longest mammal migration** (8,200 km; 5,095 mi), but also to make loud, resonant signalling sounds by "tail-slapping" the water.

How many animals can you identify on this map? See pp.186–87 for answers.

47

THE TUSKED TITAN

Adult male African elephants are the **largest living land animals**. They stand up to 3.7 m (12 ft) at the shoulder and can weigh 7 tonnes (15,432 lb) – more than 100 men!

An elephant uses its trunk – the **most muscular nose** of any mammal – to smell, breathe, feel vibrations, stroke its young, drink water and hold objects, while with its tusks it digs, forages and fights. Massive ears help to offload excess heat, and can express aggression or joy by flapping. Used together with the soles of its feet and trunk, they also detect sound over vast distances – hearing calls as far away as 10 km (6.2 mi) under ideal conditions.

52

LITTLE & LARGE

CA 781-118

58

LITTLE & LARGE

LARGEST VS SMALLEST MAMMAL

All mammals have backbones, warm-blooded bodies and offspring fed on milk. But when it comes to size, the variation couldn't be more extreme...

BLUE WHALE

SCIENTIFIC NAME: *Balaenoptera musculus*

TYPE: Mammal

LENGTH: Up to 33.58 m (110 ft 2 in)

WEIGHT: Up to 190 tonnes (418,880 lb)

DIET: Filter feeder, e.g., krill, copepods

LIFESPAN: 80–90 years

RANGE: All oceans except the Arctic

AVERAGE LENGTH

AVERAGE WEIGHT

IN SCALE

LARGEST MAMMAL

The **largest animal ever** – dwarfing even the biggest dinosaurs (see pp.92–113) – is the blue whale. The epic proportions of this mighty marine mammal have seen it dominate the natural-world record books. It has the **largest heart** and **largest nose**, as well as the **heaviest tongue**. Even a baby blue whale – the animal kingdom's **largest offspring** – is about the same weight as a fully grown rhino!

4–8
BEATS PER MINUTE
The blue whale has the slowest heart rate for a mammal

188 dB
Blue whales (and their cousins the fin whales) make the loudest animal calls

450 m
The farthest glide by a mammal, achieved by a giant flying squirrel (1,475 ft)

220
MYA
Millions of years ago that the first mammal – the shrew-like *Adelobasileus cromptoni* – lived

120 ms
The speed at which a star-nosed mole can catch and eat prey; it's the fastest eater among mammals

AVERAGE LENGTH

AVERAGE WEIGHT

IN SCALE

50x

BUMBLEBEE BAT

SCIENTIFIC NAME: *Craseonycteris thonglongyai*

TYPE: Mammal

LENGTH: Up to 3.3 cm (1.2 in)

WEIGHT: Up to 2 g (0.07 oz)

DIET: Insectivore, e.g., small flies

LIFESPAN: 5–10 years (estimated)

RANGE: Thailand and Myanmar (Burma)

SMALLEST MAMMAL

Given its bug-sized body, it's easy to see how the bumblebee bat got its name. Discovered only in the 1970s, this tiny creature – aka the Kitti's hog-nosed bat – lives in limestone caves in the bamboo forests of south-east Asia. It emerges to hunt at dawn and dusk, using ultrasonic squeaks to both detect prey and avoid collisions in the low light.

A blue whale can be how many times heavier than a bumblebee bat? a) 3 million; b) 95 million; c) 1 billion

LITTLE & LARGE

ALL ABOUT POLAR BEARS

They might look cuddly from a distance, but "snow bears" are made of tough stuff, ruling over their frozen realm with superlative senses and fierce endurance.

It's hard to imagine a polar bear cub ever being anything other than adorable... But these Arctic apex predators grow up to be the world's **largest bears**. On their hind legs, adult males can stand taller than a telephone box and weigh the same as a grand piano!

With a dense fur coat, stores of fat and massive paws that act like snow-shoes, they're perfectly adapted for life in the freezer. In the Arctic Circle where they live, the mercury can plummet to an average -34°C (-29°F) during the long winter months.

Snow bears are as at home in water as on land; they can swim for days between islands or sea-ice. As polar temperatures continue to rise, so do the distances that these hardy animals have to travel to seek food.

WHERE IN THE WORLD?

CHURCHILL, CANADA

Known as the "polar bear capital of the world", this remote little town in Manitoba, Canada, has been one of the top destinations for polar bear sightings for decades. The best season to see them here is in the autumn (Oct/Nov). At this time, many bears venture from inland towards the shore of Hudson Bay in anticipation of the sea freezing over.

NOSE
Polar bears are able to sniff out a seal more than 30 km (18 mi) away! It's the **most sensitive nose for a land mammal**.

BLUBBER
Combined with its thick fur, a 10-cm-thick (3.9-in) layer of fat beneath the skin provides polar bears with the **most efficient insulation in a bear**.

PADDLE PAWS
The huge front feet are slightly webbed, making them perfect for swimming between ice floes.

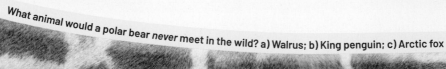

What animal would a polar bear never meet in the wild? a) Walrus; b) King penguin; c) Arctic fox

MEET THE FAMILY

The brown bear is the **bear with the most subspecies**. It has 15 types globally – from the Himalayas to the Rockies.

South America's spectacled bears eat everything from birds, deer and rabbits to fruit, honey and cacti. Among bear-kind, they have the **most varied diet.**

The **smallest bear species** is the sun bear of south-east Asia. One polar bear weighs roughly the same as six sun bears!

SNOW-GOGGLE EYES

Special membranes help to counter UV radiation; these built-in shades provide protection from dazzling sunlight and snow-blindness.

ON THE HUNT

For the Arctic's top predator, meals are few and far between. Seals are their main prey and they have developed a variety of ways to hunt them. These include waiting patiently by a breathing hole for an unwitting seal to come up for air and swimming out to icebergs where seals like to rest. They also break into seals' birthing chambers, which can be 1 m (3 ft 3 in) beneath the snow!

SEE-THROUGH FUR

A polar bear's hair isn't white – it's hollow and transparent. It appears white because of the way light refracts through it. This allows sunlight to pass through and be absorbed by the bear's black skin, keeping it warm.

9 Days straight that a radio-collared female polar bear swam for, covering a record distance of 426 mi (685 km) in 2008!

SUPER-LIVER

A polar bear's seal-based diet is rich in vitamin A. Its liver stores so much that, if eaten by a human, it can cause hypervitaminosis A, with symptoms including bone pain and blurry vision.

POLAR BEAR

SCIENTIFIC NAME: *Ursus maritimus*

TYPE: Mammal

LENGTH: 2.4–2.6 m (7 ft 10 in–8 ft 6 in)

WEIGHT: 400–600 kg (880–1,320 lb)

DIET: Carnivore, e.g., seals

LIFESPAN: 4–8 years

RANGE: Arctic Circle

LARGEST VS SMALLEST BIRD

While all birds today have beaks and wings, these direct dinosaur descendants have diversified almost beyond belief, as demonstrated by these two winged wonders.

LARGEST BIRD

Ostriches are the biggest of the "ratites": flightless birds whose family includes emus, kiwis and cassowaries (see pp.118–19). But size isn't this species' only superlative quality. They're also the **fastest birds on land**, hitting speeds of 72 km/h (45 mph) – about the same as a greyhound. Sprinting away is their default response to danger, though they can also deliver a nasty kick with legs powerful enough to kill a lion.

AVERAGE HEIGHT

EGG SIZE

Largest bird egg (living species)

IN SCALE

OSTRICH

SCIENTIFIC NAME: *Struthio camelus*

TYPE: Bird

HEIGHT: Up to 2.7 m (9 ft)

WEIGHT: Up to 156.5 kg (345 lb)

DIET: Omnivore, e.g., roots, fruit, insects, lizards

LIFESPAN: 30–40 years

RANGE: Sub-Saharan Africa

5 cm

Diameter of an ostrich's eyeball – the largest eyes for a land animal (2 in)

80

The most birds mimicked by a bird, achieved by the marsh warbler

40 g

Weight of the smallest living flightless bird: the Inaccessible Island rail, native to a remote island in the Atlantic (1.4 oz)

300
NESTS

Several hundred sociable weavers flock together to build the most populous communal bird nests

42 km/h

Top speed of North America's roadrunner, the fastest-running flying bird (26 mph). Meep, meep!

AVERAGE LENGTH

EGG SIZE

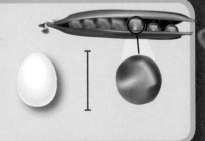

IN SCALE

10x

SMALLEST BIRD

At the other end of the avian scale is the tiny bee hummingbird, which weighs less than a penny and is only a little wider than a credit card. These Caribbean natives are as busy as their buzzy namesakes. They can beat their wings more than 80 times per second, making them ace aviators, able to hover in one place or even fly backwards. All of that activity demands a high-energy diet, though; they need to eat about half their body weight in nectar every day!

100%

BEE HUMMINGBIRD

SCIENTIFIC NAME: *Mellisuga helenae*

TYPE: Bird

LENGTH: 5.7 cm (2.2 in)

WEIGHT: 1.6 g (0.05 oz)

DIET: Nectarivore, i.e., nectar

LIFESPAN: 7–10 years

RANGE: Cuba and the Isle of Youth

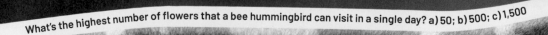
What's the highest number of flowers that a bee hummingbird can visit in a single day? a) 50; b) 500; c) 1,500

LARGEST VS SMALLEST REPTILE

The first reptiles evolved more than 300 million years ago. Maybe that begins to explain the mind-boggling variety of scaly species we've discovered so far...

LONGEST REPTILE

Based on length, reticulated pythons are the largest reptiles. They typically grow to around 6.2 m (20 ft 4 in), but one super-sized serpent, measured at 10 m (32 ft 9.7 in) in 1912, holds the record for the longest specimen.

An "ambush predator", this snake comes armed with more than 100 teeth, which it uses to grab and hold fast its prey. It then suffocates the helpless victim with its muscular body and swallows it whole – even if it's a deer with antlers!

RETICULATED PYTHON

SCIENTIFIC NAME: *Python reticulatus*

TYPE: Reptile

LENGTH: 6.2 m (20 ft 4 in)

WEIGHT: Up to 181 kg (400 lb)

DIET: Carnivore, e.g., rats, pigs, primates, deer

LIFESPAN: 20–25 years

RANGE: South-east Asia

AVERAGE LENGTH

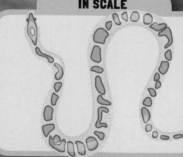

AVERAGE WEIGHT

IN SCALE

34.9
KM/H
Top speed of a spiny-tailed iguana, the fastest lizard (21.6 mph)

92 dB
Top volume of the noisiest crocodilian – the American alligator

315
MILLION YEARS
Age of the oldest reptile fossils: *Hylonomus* bones from the Bay of Fundy in Canada

1,200 kg
Weight of a male saltwater crocodile, the heaviest reptile (2,645 lb) – that's about two-and-a-half grand pianos!

13–15
MONTHS
The longest reptile egg incubation, that of New Zealand's tuatara

AVERAGE LENGTH

SMALLEST REPTILE

There are some 160 species of chameleon, many of them found only on the African island of Madagascar. Three species of dwarf leaf chameleon – the minute leaf, the micro leaf and the Mount d'Ambre leaf chameleons (the latter is pictured here) – measure just 1.4 cm (0.5 in) from the snout to the end of the body. Each one is tiny enough to fit on a human thumbnail!

AVERAGE WEIGHT

IN SCALE

25x

LEAF CHAMELEON

SCIENTIFIC NAME: *Brookesia tuberculata*

TYPE: Reptile

LENGTH: 1.4 cm (0.5 in)

WEIGHT: 0.18 g (0.006 oz) (estimate)

DIET: Insectivore, e.g., ants, fruit flies

LIFESPAN: 10 years (estimate)

RANGE: Madagascar

To ambush a nest-building heron, the mugger crocodile... a) Balances sticks on its head; b) Imitates heron calls; c) Hides in IKEA

MINI BEASTS

They may not be the biggest, fastest or strongest, but these tiny critters – often masters of hide-and-seek – still have superpowers to spare.

SMALLEST OWL

The elf owl from south-western USA and Mexico is about 12–14 cm (4.7–5.5 in) long and weighs about the same as a golf ball. With a wingspan of only 27 cm (10.6 in), an adult can easily be mistaken for an owlet. The tiny nocturnal birds sometimes play dead to avoid danger, yet in small groups have been known to mob creatures that are many times their own size!

SMALLEST CHELONIAN

The shell of the speckled cape tortoise, or speckled padloper, is about 6–9.6 cm (2.3–3.7 in) long. "Padloper" means "path runner", and refers to the South African trails where the reptile is often found. Its diminutive size allows it to escape predators by hiding in the cracks and crevices along those dry, rocky paths.

SMALLEST MARSUPIAL

Excluding its tail, the long-tailed planigale – aka the flat-skulled marsupial mouse – is only about 5 cm (1.9 in) long. Found in Australia's grasslands, where there is a long dry season, the minuscule creature hides from predators and hunts for other small animals in deep cracks in the ground.

Smallest owl

I'm a firm believer that the best things come in small packages!

1 cm (0.39 in)

Smallest chelonian

PUNIER THAN A PENNY!

At just 7 mm (0.27 in) from snout to vent, the **smallest frog** is Papua New Guinea's *Paedophryne amauensis*. See more on this mini Kermit on p.67.

Parasitic pea crabs – the **smallest crabs** – have shells that measure no more than 6.3 mm (0.24 in) across. They live inside molluscs such as oysters.

The **smallest starfish** is the asterinid sea star, discovered off South Australia in 1975. It spans just 9 mm (0.35 in) at its widest.

DID YOU KNOW?

Shrews are some of the tiniest mammals. The Eurasian pygmy shrew, at 4 cm (1.5 in), is the **smallest land mammal**, while its cousin the American water shrew (13 cm; 5 in) scoops the award for **smallest aquatic mammal**.

I'm feeling a little horse today...

SMALLEST WOODPECKER

The bar-breasted piculet measures no more than 7.5 cm (2.9 in) long and weighs a mere 10 g (0.3 oz) – about the same as two grapes! It lives on the edges of humid lowland forests in South America. Owing to their size, very little is known about their lifestyle.

SMALLEST NEWT

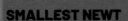

Newts are a type of salamander and the Mexican lungless salamander is the smallest at just 2.5 cm (1 in) – and that's *including* its tail! Salamanders often have dull camouflage colouring. Others, like this little dazzler, send a big message to predators in spite of their tiny size: a hi-vis warning that they're toxic to eat!

SMALLEST SEA HORSE

A Satomi's pygmy sea horse, at just 13.8 mm (0.5 in) long, is about the size of a thumbnail and has been mistaken for the offspring of another species. Described in 2008, it lives in the tropical reefs around Derawan Island, which lies off Indonesian Borneo.

8
Species of pygmy sea horse that have been discovered to date (one is yet to be named). The first one was spotted only in 1969.

1 cm (0.39 in)

100%

Smallest marsupial

Smallest woodpecker

Smallest newt

Smallest sea horse

How many pecks per second does a woodpecker peck? a) 150; b) 7.5; c) 20

LARGEST VS SMALLEST FISH

They're both fish, but that's where the similarities end. Whale sharks can be 3,000 times longer – and up to 3 million times heavier! – than their diminutive deep-sea cousins.

WHALE SHARK

SCIENTIFIC NAME: *Rhincodon typus*

TYPE: Fish

LENGTH: Up to 18.8 m (61 ft 8 in)

WEIGHT: Up to 30 tonnes (66,138 lb)

DIET: Filter feeder, e.g., plankton, fish eggs

LIFESPAN: 70–100 years

RANGE: Global, but prefers tropical waters

LARGEST FISH

The whale shark is a gentle giant. While its predatory cousins terrorize the oceans, it lives on a diet of plankton – like a blue whale. A typical adult whale shark measures 9–12 m (29–39 ft) in length, but there are reports of supersized specimens reaching double the lower limit of that range! Despite their size, whale sharks are hard to track, so we know very little about their behaviour.

AVERAGE LENGTH

6
EYES
Six-eyed spookfish from the depths of the Pacific are the fish with the most eyes

109
KM/H
Top speed of the fastest fish, the sailfish (68 mph)

0.016
KM/H
Top speed of the slowest fish, the dwarf sea horse (0.001 mph)

2 mg
The dwarf goby is the lightest fish (0.00007 oz); it would take 28,500 to match the weight of a tennis ball!

5.2 km
Tibetan loaches of the Himalayas are the highest-living fish (3.2 mi)

ANGLERFISH

SCIENTIFIC NAME: *Photocorynus spiniceps*

TYPE: Fish

LENGTH: 6.2 mm (0.24 in)

WEIGHT: <10 g (<0.35 oz)

DIET: Parasite (absorbs nutrients from female host)

LIFESPAN: Unknown

RANGE: Atlantic and Pacific oceans

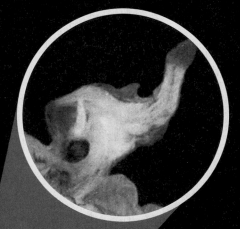

SMALLEST FISH

Most male anglerfish are small, but the smallest – *Photocorynus spiniceps* – reaches a minuscule 6.2 mm (0.24 in) long, compared with 46-mm (1.8-in) females. That also makes them the **smallest vertebrates** overall. Each male swims around in the gloomy ocean depths until he meets a female, then fuses himself to her back, living off his partner for the rest of his life.

IN SCALE

50x

Which of these is a real shark species? a) Monster shark; b) Megamouth shark; c) Spaniel shark

100%

BIG PICTURE

TINY TABBY

With a head-and-body length of just 35–48 cm (14–19 in), the rusty-spotted cat is the **smallest wild cat**. Native to southern India and Sri Lanka, it's closely related to the Asian leopard cat. A skilful climber and fierce hunter, it stalks at night – sometimes in trees as well as on the ground.

IT'S ALL RELATIVE!

The **newest wild cat** to be officially recognized is the southern Brazilian oncilla, in 2013. Because oncillas – or "tigrinas" – from Brazil's Atlantic forest don't interbreed with any others in the country, they're now considered to be a separate species.

SUB-SIZE TO SUBSTANTIAL

METRES

Rusty-spotted cat
Domestic cat
Tiger

0 1 2 3 4 5

An average pet cat, tipping the scales at 4 kg (8 lb 13 oz), is about two-and-a-half times as heavy as the 1.6-kg (3-lb 8-oz) rusty-spotted cat. A tiger, meanwhile, at a massive 261 kg (575 lb), weighs about the same as 163 "rusties"!

60 G

A newborn rusty-spotted kitten weighs the same as a tennis ball (2.1 oz)!

Not all cats hate water! Which cats swim – and even dive – to keep cool and chase prey? a) Bobtails; b) Balinese bathing cats; c) Tigers

LITTLE & LARGE

LARGEST vs SMALLEST AMPHIBIAN

Minute and perfectly camouflaged in its leaf-litter home, the tiniest amphibian is hard to spot. Its super-sized cousin, on the other hand, is pretty hard to miss!

LARGEST AMPHIBIAN

Chinese giant salamanders live in mountain streams and lakes in central China. They spend their whole lives in water-filled cavities on muddy and rocky banks, taking in oxygen through their skin. Having poor eyesight, they detect prey by sensing vibrations in the water. One record-breaking specimen measured about the same length as an adult man!

AVERAGE LENGTH

AVERAGE WEIGHT

IN SCALE

CHINESE GIANT SALAMANDER

SCIENTIFIC NAME: *Andrias davidianus*

TYPE: Amphibian

LENGTH: Up to 1.8 m (5 ft 11 in)

WEIGHT: Up to 65 kg (143 lb)

DIET: Carnivore, e.g., frogs, shrimp, worms, insects

LIFESPAN: 60–70 years

RANGE: China

66

−18 °C

Temperature endured by wood frogs (−0.4°F). They're the most cold-resistant amphibians

2 m

Distance the first known poison-squirting toads – Amazonian toads – can project poison from behind their eyes (6 ft 6 in)

35 THOUSAND

Eggs laid by the female cane toad, the most eggs per spawning for a frog/toad

1.58 m

Length of the longest Chinese giant salamander specimen – living (5 ft 2 in), Karlo. He resides at Prague Zoo in the Czech Republic

4 kg

Weight of the heaviest frog ever, *Beelzebubo ampinga* (8 lb 13 oz). It dates from 65–100 million years ago

AVERAGE LENGTH

AVERAGE WEIGHT

IN SCALE

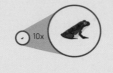

AMAU FROG

SCIENTIFIC NAME: *Paedophryne amauensis*

TYPE: Amphibian

LENGTH: 7.7 mm (0.3 in)

WEIGHT: 0.02 g (0.0007 oz)

DIET: Insectivore

LIFESPAN: Unknown

RANGE: Papua New Guinea

SMALLEST AMPHIBIAN

The puny *Paedophryne amauensis* – seen above sitting on a dime that's just 1.7 cm (0.7 in) across – eats tiny invertebrates such as mites that are ignored by bigger predators. The earth-coloured frog lives in leaf litter on New Guinea's rainforest floor, and is reported to be a fantastically good jumper — able to leap up to 30 times its own body length!

A giant salamander's child-like cries led to its nickname... a) Baby fish; b) Wailing newt; c) Sobbing salamander

ON THE MAP

EUROPE

From the frozen north to the balmy Mediterranean Sea, a bounty of wildlife calls this continent home.

Most widely distributed owl

15 The common barn owl's near-global range is estimated at 63.3 million km² (24.4 million sq mi). Antarctica is the only continent it doesn't inhabit. It hunts at night: even in total darkness it can find the smallest scurrying rodent using its super-sensitive hearing.

Largest grouse

19 Male western capercaillies, which live in the pine forests of northern Europe, can weigh 4 kg (8 lb 13 oz); the females are roughly half that size. In the spring, the males are famed for their outlandish and noisy courtship dance, known as a "lek".

Most endangered wild cat

21 The Iberian lynx, smaller than its Eurasian cousin but with the same bobbed tail, lives only in Spain and Portugal. Conservation projects are helping to restore its numbers: the latest 2015 census showed the total had quadrupled to 404 in 13 years.

68

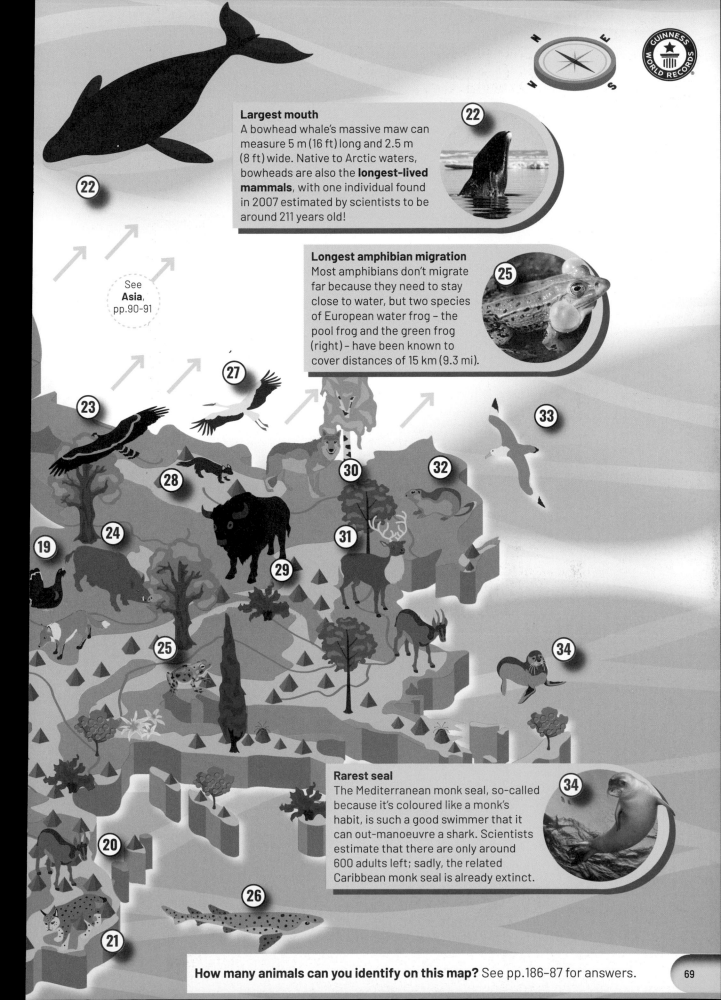

Largest mouth

A bowhead whale's massive maw can measure 5 m (16 ft) long and 2.5 m (8 ft) wide. Native to Arctic waters, bowheads are also the **longest-lived mammals**, with one individual found in 2007 estimated by scientists to be around 211 years old!

Longest amphibian migration

Most amphibians don't migrate far because they need to stay close to water, but two species of European water frog – the pool frog and the green frog (right) – have been known to cover distances of 15 km (9.3 mi).

See **Asia**, pp.90–91

Rarest seal

The Mediterranean monk seal, so-called because it's coloured like a monk's habit, is such a good swimmer that it can out-manoeuvre a shark. Scientists estimate that there are only around 600 adults left; sadly, the related Caribbean monk seal is already extinct.

How many animals can you identify on this map? See pp.186–87 for answers.

LEADING LIGHTS

The ability to light up is a pretty dazzling talent, especially if you can shine 90% more efficiently than a light bulb! The luminous cucujo (inset right) is the **most bioluminescent insect**. It's part of the firefly family, which is actually comprised entirely of beetles. The brilliant yellow flashes are triggered by chemicals reacting in the body. In other lightning bugs, these produce red and green lights.

82

CREEPY-CRAWLIES

80

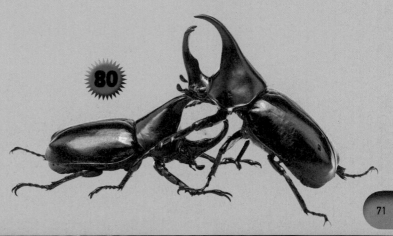

CREEPY-CRAWLIES

STING IN THE TAIL

Bees, ants and scorpions have evolved a special weapon that comes in as handy for defence as it does attack. Here, we celebrate some of nature's super stingers!

EMPEROR SCORPION

The **heaviest scorpion** is the large black West African emperor scorpion, which can weigh more than a tennis ball. It's about the size of a human hand. It uses its strong pincers to kill most prey, keeping the stinger for larger quarry or for self-defence.

BUGS TO LIFE!

GO TO PP. 88-89

TARANTULA HAWK WASP

At 6 cm (2.4 in) long, tarantula hawks are the **largest wasps** and a spider's worst nightmare... A female paralyses a tarantula with her sting, then drags it back to her nest. There, she lays an egg on the spider's body and seals the nest, where the baby wasp will feed on the still-living victim. *Yikes!*

AFRICANIZED HONEY BEE

Although their venom is no more potent than that of other bees, these are considered the **most dangerous bees** for two reasons. One, they attack in big swarms, and two, they pursue victims over great distances (see left).

0.4 KM

Distance that Africanized honey bees have been known to chase people who ventured too close to their nests (0.2 mi)!

72

The **smallest scorpion** – *Microbuthus pusillus* – measures a minute 13 mm (0.8 in). It's found on coasts around the Red Sea.

Scorpions don't only live in deserts... The UK hosts a colony of European yellow-tailed scorpions. They have lived on the dockland walls of Sheerness in Kent since the 1700s.

Under UV light, many scorpions glow an amazing aqua colour, owing to certain proteins in their shells. As to *why* they do this, it's debated. Theories include that it helps them to detect moonlight or to deflect the Sun's rays.

BULLDOG ANT

You'll want to give the bulldog ant, found in coastal regions of Australia, a wide berth! During attack, it uses its stinger and jaws simultaneously. It's been responsible for at least three human deaths since 1936, which makes it the **most dangerous ant**.

FAT-TAILED SCORPION

Fat-tailed scorpions are the **most venomous scorpions** on the planet. The Tunisian fat-tail (below), for instance, can kill a human with just 18.2 mg (0.0006 oz) of venom! The species accounts for as much as 90% of all scorpion fatalities in northern Africa.

RED VELVET ANT

Despite its name and appearance, this colourful bug is actually a wasp. The females of this species have fuzzy bodies and no wings, hence why they're often mistaken for ants. They're also known as "cow killers" because, as the legend goes, their sting is so painful that it's enough to make a cow pass out!

Turn over to meet the "King of Sting", Dr Justin Schmidt!

Which type of bees are unable to sting? a) Drones; b) Workers; c) Queens

INTERVIEW
THE KING OF STING

Entomologist Justin Schmidt has lost track of how many times he has been stung during his career working with insects. But he has put the pain to good use...

Bug scientist Justin Schmidt was curious to discover more about the effects of insect stings. So in 1983 he developed the Schmidt Sting Pain Index to measure the painfulness of different animals' stings. The index runs from "1" (mild) to "4" (severe).

⚡: Our "sting symbol" shows the pain rating Dr Schmidt has allocated to some of the insects shown here.

Why did you develop the index?
I wanted to find out whether the most painful stings are also the ones that can do the most damage. We could already measure the damage a sting inflicts by a variety of different methods, but we had no meaningful way to measure the pain.

How does the index work?
The index records how much pain an insect sting causes so that we can make scientific comparisons between different species' stings. I chose the four-point scale because it's hard to distinguish between levels of pain in finer detail – on a 10-point scale, say.

Do you go out of your way to get stung, or is it unavoidable?
I usually get stung in the process of studying a particular insect species.

Only very rarely do I have to provoke a sting, and in those cases – when the insect is unwilling to sting – the sting isn't very painful.

Has your pain threshold for stings increased over the years?
No!

Which sting most surprised you?
Several surprised me. Most were surprising because they didn't hurt as much as I expected. Based on reports of other scientists and early explorers, I assumed that the matabele and giant stink ants of Africa, the bulldog ants of Australia and especially the slender twig ant from Asia would be hugely painful. None of these hurt nearly as much as I'd anticipated.

One that hurt *more* than I expected was an ordinary honey bee – but that was when it flew into my mouth and stung my tongue!

Why do you think your research has captured the public's imagination?
We are fascinated by things that are not life-threatening but still intimidate us or cause us apprehension. But some fears go deeper, and are seemingly imprinted

in our DNA. Perhaps this fear is rooted in our prehistoric ancestors' interactions with stinging insects and other potentially dangerous animals.

The Asian giant hornet is the **largest species of hornet** – its stinger alone can reach 0.6 cm (0.2 in) long! Pain doesn't always equate to size, though; it's only rated as a "2" on the index.

Why do people seem to love bees but hate wasps?
We love honey bees for historical reasons associated with their honey: until relatively recently, honey was one of very few sources of sweetness. Honey bees are now also known to be important pollinators of our food crops.

Wasps are less well loved mainly because they don't provide anything like honey – but they still sting! They are highly beneficial to us, though, because they prey on flies that bite and cause disease as well as on caterpillars that eat our crops.

Do you travel a lot as an entomologist?
I do. On one of my most memorable trips, I arrived at a

THE ULTIMATE STING

The **most painful insect sting**, registering 4+, is that of the bullet ant, native to Central America and South America. Schmidt describes the sensation as "like walking over flaming charcoal with a three-inch rusty nail in your heel"! Others have likened the pain to a gunshot wound – hence the insect's common name.

STUNG TO DEATH: How many stings could kill a human*?

POLYBIA WASP
2,780

TARANTULA HAWK WASPS

1,250–5,000

877

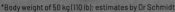
HONEY BEE

BUMBLEBEE

278

794

BULLET ANT

*Body weight of 50 kg (110 lb); estimates by Dr Schmidt

Here, Dr Schmidt searches for 1.8-cm-long (0.7-in) Amazon termite-raiding ants in the rainforest near Belém, Brazil.

caravan camp in Limpopo, South Africa, to discover a great wealth of insects everywhere in the beautiful park grounds. There were huge predacious ground beetles, myriad amazing velvet ants, astonishing giant velvet mites and even the occasional "big and hairy", such as a serval [a type of wild cat].

What's the best thing about being an entomologist?
The best thing is that you get to study some really cool creatures and make fascinating discoveries about them. Insects are everywhere and are so important – not only to our physical health and well-being, but also to our mental health and

To find out more about Justin O Schmidt's Sting Pain Index, check out his book, *The Sting of the Wild*. As well as the worst culprits, you'll also learn about insect anatomy and their motives for stinging.

The Story of the Man Who Got Stung for Science
THE STING OF THE WILD
JUSTIN O. SCHMIDT
Johns Hopkins University Press

enjoyment of the world. One funny thing about being an entomologist is that some people confuse us with etymologists [those who study the origins of words]. I often wonder if etymologists also get confused with us!

What does a typical "day at the office" involve for you?
If I have some scientific writing to do, that comes first, when my brain is freshest. After that, I tend to the animals, conduct laboratory research, read scientific literature and maybe take a walk in the dry wash behind the lab. Then back to preparing for lectures and planning the next day's activities. Actually, there's no such thing as a typical day!

Tell us an interesting fact about ants that not many people know.
Ants have been used in coming-of-age rituals by indigenous peoples throughout much of the world – especially in the New World.

Which of your sting descriptions are you most proud of?
One of my favourites is the Florida harvester ant, which, though it's not aggressive and almost has to be forced to sting someone, still achieves a "3" on the index. I describe the pain as: "Bold and unrelenting. Somebody is using a power drill to excavate your ingrown toenail." The club-horned wasp, on the other hand, which doesn't even merit a "1", is: "Disappointing. A paper clip falls on your bare foot."

Finally, what could the human race learn from insects?
We're all in this tiny little place we call Earth and we all need each other. At least we need the insects, though I'm not so sure that very many of them need us! Be kind and tolerant of other life forms, including insects – they benefit us and make our lives richer.

What? Have I got something on my face?

Which brave bird has been seen taking on tarantula hawk wasps? a) Ostrich; b) Roadrunner; c) Woodpecker

GUINNESS WORLD RECORDS

WORM CHARMING

Once the serious business of bait-hunting fishermen, coaxing earthworms from the ground by mimicking nature has now become an international sport.

Come on, guys –
get a wriggle on –
I only need another
136 to win!

At the World Worm Charming Championships in Willaston, Cheshire, UK, teams compete to collect the most worms from their designated patch of ground in 30 min. Most contestants draw them up by imitating rain, when these critters naturally surface to avoid drowning. Rain is faked by splashing liquid on to the ground or digging in a garden tool and vibrating ("fiddling") it....

Some take the "charm" approach more literally, hoping to entice the worms with music....

WILD WORM CHARMERS

Sensing the vibrations made by approaching moles, worms flee upwards, to escape the furry predators.

Seagulls "dance", stamping each foot in turn to generate vibrations similar to those made by rain. Worms burrow upward to avoid being flooded.

Stomping the ground with their feet, wood turtles too have learned how to drum up an easy meal.

A CHARMING FAMILY

The Love-Rouse family from Willaston (above) won the 38th World Worm Charming Championships in 2017, collecting a total of 137 worms.

The **most worms charmed** ever is 567, by 10-year-old Sophie Smith (UK) in 2009. Hopeful charmers come from far and wide – including India, South Africa and the USA – to compete.

POSTERIOR (BACK)

CILIA
Tiny bristle-like protrusions on the worm's underside help it to grip the soil.

SADDLE
This thick, unsegmented band secretes a glue-like mucus that protects the worm's eggs.

What internal organ do earthworms lack? a) Heart; b) Intestine; c) Lungs

The rules of the official worm charming federation specify that charmers have a 3-m² (32-sq-ft) plot and a brief warm-up period. All worms must be returned to the ground after an event, unharmed.

Worms like damp conditions, but will drown in waterlogged soil. Some competitors encourage them to surface by sprinkling the ground with water, tea or even beer!

Judges tally up the worms before the winner is announced.

SEGMENTS
An earthworm has about 100–150 body segments, each of which is ringed with muscle.

Teams often include a charmer and a catcher, as well as a counter.

PROSTOMIUM
Having no eyes, ears, nose or hands, worms use a lip-like flap over the mouth to sense their environment.

ANTERIOR (FRONT)

A garden fork is always a popular tool among charmers.

MOUTH
Special sensory cells in the mouth recognize different chemicals, helping the worm to "taste" its food.

WONDER WEBS

Why bother chasing after your dinner when you can let it come to you? Spiders have been using sticky silk to weave both their traps and homes for millennia.

FIRST WEBS IN SPACE

Two female cross spiders, called Anita and Arabella, made one huge step for arachnid-kind when they ventured into space in 1973. They were launched to the US *Skylab* space station (inset right) to investigate how zero-g conditions would affect their web-building abilities. It turns out that weightlessness makes no difference to the web's structure; however, the silk was slightly finer and more inconsistent than that made on Earth.

In 2010, widespread flooding in Pakistan led to many spiders (among other bugs) taking to the trees for refuge. The result was some spectacular scenes like this, with trees almost totally cocooned in silk. One of the upsides of this amazing phenomenon was a drast reduction in the local mosquito population, which led to fewer cas of malaria (see pp.120–21 for more about the **deadliest animals**).

TYPES OF WEB

The classic design that most of us imagine is the wheel-like "orb web". The "spokes" are used by the spider to get around.

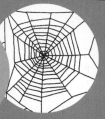

A "funnel web" is coated in adhesive silk, creating a trap with a large surface area. This design also provides a handy place for the owner of the web to hide.

A "cobweb" may look messy, but there is method to the chaos. A struggling insect quickly gets tangled up in this sticky trap.

OMG!

Weight for weight, spider silk can be five times stronger than steel!

STRONGEST SPIDER SILK

Only discovered in 2001, the Darwin's bark spider of Madagascar is believed to build the toughest webs of any arachnid. Its silk is around 10 times more robust than Kevlar – the material used in bulletproof vests! This strength comes from the silk's elasticity; it can stretch a long way before it snaps.

These spiders construct orb-shaped webs that can span 25 m (82 ft) over rivers, making them also the **longest webs**.

This chunk of amber, unearthed in Spain, contains a wasp, beetle, mite and fly ensnared in prehistoric spider silk. It's the **oldest spider web with trapped prey**, dating back 110 million years to the Early Cretaceous.

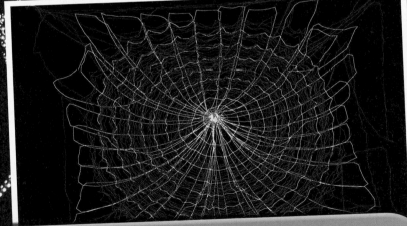

When constructing a web with sticky silk, spiders have to be careful or risk becoming tangled in their own trap!

The above colour-coded image shows some of the key elements in an orb-shaped web. The first stage involves laying down "anchor threads" (red) to give a structural outline by bridging gaps between sturdy objects in the environment such as branches. Next, the "spokes" (yellow) complete the main framework. A temporary spiral thread (white) gives structural integrity to the radial lines (though this may later be destroyed). Finally, the "catching spiral" (blue), coated in drops of natural glue, is laid.

Which of these weapons does a gladiator spider create with its silk? a) Sword; b) Trident; c) Net

BEETLE MANIA!

With superhero strength, reinforced armour and galaxy-driven GPS systems, these talented little critters seem to excel in all areas...

1

My tin-opener's bust... Mind if I use yours?

2

I'm always being asked which is the lesser of two weevils!

3

4

5

BEETLE'S GOT TALENT!

Dung beetles use the light of stars in the Milky Way to help them roll their balls of poop in a straight line. That way, they don't go in circles!

The golden tortoise beetle can toggle between two different colours using a "switchable reflector" mechanism in its shell.

Trilobite beetles, which come in a range of colours, have foldable armoured plates and can retract their heads like tortoises.

Goliath beetles are also some of the strongest animals on Earth, able to lift several hundred times their own weight!

6

OMG!
One in every four animals on Earth is a beetle!

7

BUGS TO LIFE!
GO TO PP. 88–89

1 Male stag beetles use their oversized jaws like stags use their antlers: to wrestle for the best mating sites. But their pincers are useless at biting – unlike the females' jaws, which can give a sharp nip.

2 Africa's long-nosed cycad weevil has the **longest beetle snout** compared to its body size. It uses the lance-like appendage – which can be twice as long as its body – for drilling nest-holes in seeds.

3 The cicada parasite beetle, or feather-horned beetle, uses its impressive antennae to "comb" the air for signs of females that are ready to mate. Each bushy-looking feeler has 20 segments or more.

4 Ladybirds come in many colours and patterns and are often thought to be lucky. Farmers love them because each one, during its lifetime, can gobble up more than 5,000 plant-eating pests!

5 Raised ridges along a jewel beetle's shell not only provide its glinting colours, but also help water and mud to run off. The beetles' lustre at one time made them popular as brooches and ornaments.

6 Africa's goliath beetle, the **heaviest insect**, can weigh as much as an apple. Males use their Y-shaped horns in battle, while females use their wedge-shaped heads to burrow nests in the ground.

7 Horns included, the Hercules beetle is the **longest beetle**, growing as long as a human hand. Males use their horns to wrestle opponents.

The three types of dung beetle named for what they do with poop are: rollers, tunnellers and... a) Dwellers; b) Munchers; c) Face-painters

ALL ABOUT PRAYING MANTIDS

Named for their habit of standing with front legs folded as if in prayer, these cannibalistic carnivores are surely the ultimate "preying" machines!

The **heaviest praying mantis** is the giant Asian mantis, which lives in India, Myanmar, Nepal and Sri Lanka. One well-fed female is on record as weighing 9 g (0.3 oz).

Preying on other bugs – and even some small vertebrates – these insects are also cannibals; their very first meal may be a sibling! When hunting, they sit quietly with their front legs raised until some unwary insect wanders by. Then they launch a lightning-fast ambush, snagging the victim with terrifying barbed front legs... before eating it alive!

FIVE EYES

A mantis's two large eyes sense movement, while three simpler eyes located between them detect light levels.

FLEXIBLE "NECK"

The narrow thorax between the abdomen and the head allows a mantis to swivel its head through 180°, so that it can scan its surroundings.

WHERE IN THE WORLD?

WESTERN GHATS, INDIA

The hill ranges of the Western Ghats extend along the west coast of India from the River Tapti to the country's southern tip. Including tropical wet evergreen forests and grasslands, the region is one of the world's most biologically diverse. Many of the thousands of animal and plant species here are found nowhere else on the planet.

LETHAL LEGS

Long sharp spines on the forelegs help the mantis to grip its prey – as if with a fork – holding it firmly in place while it tucks into its live meal!

BUGS TO LIFE!
GO TO PP. 88-89

DID YOU KNOW?

Mantids have a single ear, located in a groove in the thorax. Ultrasonic hearing gives these insects advance warning of bats and so – hopefully – helps them to avoid becoming bat food!

THE MANTIS FAMILY

The dead leaf (or ghost) mantis has evolved to look dry and crumpled, and will hide among decaying vegetation.

The orchid mantis, found in the rainforests of south-east Asia, has taken on the colour and shape of the blooms where it lurks in wait for prey.

The flower mantis from Java, Indonesia, is the **largest mantis**. Its slender body can reach 20 cm (7.8 in) long.

FATAL ATTRACTION

After – or sometimes during! – mating, a female mantis will often bite off her partner's head and then devour him. This may seem a disastrous start to parenthood, but in fact it gives both partners reproductive advantages. If a female eats her man, she produces more than twice as many eggs; plus the meal provides more than half of her mating-season diet. The male's death, then, assures healthier offspring – even if he isn't around to see his kids grow up!

I've had better first dates...

GIANT ASIAN MANTIS

SCIENTIFIC NAME: *Hierodula membranacea*

TYPE: Insect

LENGTH: Up to 10 cm (3.9 in)

WEIGHT: 9 g (0.3 oz)

DIET: Carnivore, e.g., crickets, flies, mantids, frogs

LIFESPAN: 12–18 months

RANGE: South-east Asia

WINGS OF CHANGE

Most adult praying mantis species have two sets of wings. The outer pair serve to hide and protect the inner transparent wings that are used to fly

400

Number of mantis nymphs that can emerge from a single eggcase (aka "ootheca").

CAMO DISGUISE

Leaf-coloured camouflage is vital to the giant Asian mantis. It helps it blend in to avoid being noticed by its prey, and also makes it hard for predators such as birds, lizards and small mammals to spot.

When a flying mantis senses danger, it will... a) Close its eyes; b) Dive-bomb; c) Shoot sticky silk from its head

BIG PICTURE

100%

MEGA MOTH

With an average 30-cm (12-in) wingspan, south-east Asia's atlas moth is so big that it's often mistaken for a bird! But in spite of the size of the **largest moth** – an adult's wings are as wide as a dinner plate – it doesn't feed at all once it has emerged from its cocoon. It lives for only a few days, moving very little during the daytime to save energy for mating at night.

The moth has patterns on the tips of its wings that can look like a snake's head. When threatened, it will drop to the ground and flail around, imitating serpent-like movements in the hope of scaring predators away.

OMG!

There's a good reason why atlas moths can't eat as adults: they have no mouths!

Atlas moth caterpillars can grow up to 2.5 cm (1 in) thick and 12 cm (4.7 in) long. In preparation for the food-free adult stage, they spend every spare second eating.

IT'S ALL RELATIVE!

The rare great owlet moth – aka the white witch – from Brazil rivals the atlas moth for the title of **largest moth**. One extra-large female found in 1934 had a wingspan of 30.8 cm (12.1 in).

Which moth is named for its skull-shaped markings? a) The grey graverobber; b) The death's-head hawk; c) The Halloween howler

THE BUG HOTEL

Safe hideaways can be hard to find for wildlife, so Pete Bullen and his team set about building a top-of-the-range retreat to shelter a wide range of bugs and beyond...

To help boost insect populations, gardeners all over the world create sanctuaries for bugs. Some are as simple as an unswept pile of leaves, while others are on a much grander scale!

The Martin Mere Wetland Centre in Lancashire, UK – part of the Wildfowl & Wetlands Trust (WWT) – and its longest-serving staff member, Pete Bullen, decided to build the **largest insect house** in 2017. They succeeded with a massive 18.4 m³ (649.7 cu ft) edifice that's drawing creepy-crawly clients in their droves.

A local packaging company supplied boxes, then schoolchildren and visitors helped to convert them into the record-breaking bug abode.

So far, not so much a hotel as an air bee and bee...

The foundation "gabions" (cages filled with rocks and logs) counted towards the hotel's overall size as they too provide an excellent habitat for bugs.

Different animals use the bug hotel for different purposes. Wasps and bumblebees make nests in the gaps; ladybirds, hoverflies and snails hibernate; and spiders and lacewing larvae check in to hide.

The wider the variety of materials, shapes and sizes used in the hotel "rooms", the more diverse the range of bugs that would be tempted to move in.

720

Number of boxes that went into making the record-breaking insect hotel.

Snails need moisture to stop their bodies from drying out. In dry conditions, a snail will retract into its shell and "shut down".

The peacock butterfly's "eyespots" on each wing are such an effective deterrent that they can scare away even large birds!

Lacewings and their larvae are welcome visitors because they eat large numbers of aphids and other garden pests.

The hotel isn't exclusive to insects. Amphibians such as frogs and toads prefer cooler, less humid conditions, so are attracted to materials such as bricks and terracotta.

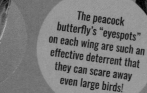

WWT Martin Mere Wetland Centre

PROFILE: PETE BULLEN, WWT

Are bug hotels a new idea?

Naturalists have always known that it's important to have undisturbed places – such as log piles – where insects can shelter. But in the 1970s and '80s, urban wildlife groups in the UK and elsewhere became more popular, so people started to make bug houses on a smaller scale.

Tell us why insect houses/hotels are so important.

They provide safe places for all kinds of smaller creatures to shelter, hibernate, lay eggs and rear young, hide from predators and hunt for prey. For example, the handsome yellow-and-black wood wasp (actually a harmless sawfly) lays its eggs in old standing timber such as poplar, and the larvae live in the wood for several years before emerging as adults. Many old trees have been removed for safety reasons, so log piles – of the right sort of wood, of course – are a vital replacement.

Do you have an insect house in your own garden?

Of course – I actually have a few! Various piles of twigs, compost piles, neglected corners and twig bundles all make for perfect habitats.

Gathering the materials and helping to construct the hotel served to engage lasting interest in the habitat project.

What do you need to build your own insect house? Can you use recycled materials?

The bugs don't mind what materials you use, but go for variety: hole size, material, height and which way the structure faces. Find a sheltered spot that gets some direct sunlight, and your guests will start to arrive...

How do you maintain an insect house?

The best advice is often to leave it alone, as it will become more natural with age.

How was your record-breaking insect hotel constructed?

The foundation was made from wire baskets filled with stone, brick and tiles, which keep the base dry. We chose a cross design so that each side would get different amounts of sunlight and rain, but it would all still be protected from the wind. Local schoolchildren helped to fill the cardboard boxes that slotted into the framework. A waterproof roof protects the structure.

How did it feel to break the record?

The whole project has been a great success in getting people involved in something practical that benefits local wildlife.

Does the WWT have plans to try any more wildlife-based records?

We may come up with new ideas – watch this space!

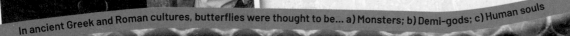

In ancient Greek and Roman cultures, butterflies were thought to be... a) Monsters; b) Demi-gods; c) Human souls

BUGS TO LIFE!

Through the technical wizardry of augmented reality (AR), see five record-breaking bugs appear out of the page. Watch out for that scorpion!

SCAN ME!

HERCULES BEETLE

This bug wasn't named after a demi-god for nothing... In terms of length, it's the **largest beetle**, reaching the same size as four LEGO® Minifigures in a row! (That's including its prodigious upper horn.) This giant member of the rhinoceros beetle clan dwells in the rainforests of Central and South America. It's beaten in weight only by the goliath beetle from Africa; see both species on p.81.

WHAT YOU'LL NEED...

To see all these mini-beasts come to life, you'll first need a connected device such as a smartphone or a tablet. Next, check the device has some space available and download the free *AugmentifyIt®* app from the App Store (iOS), Google Play (Android) or Amazon Appstore. For speed, it's worth doing this over wi-fi.

Once the app is downloaded, it's as simple as opening it, then holding the built-in camera steadily over one of the bugs. After a few seconds, you'll see a loading wheel appear. Let the app do its work and watch as the creepy-crawly transforms from 2D to 3D on the screen! Then why not test your knowledge with the built-in mini quizzes? To activate another critter, simply block the camera or move it away, then repeat the process.

AUGMENTIFY IT.

VIETNAMESE CENTIPEDE

Scurrying through tropical and subtropical forests and grasslands worldwide, this is one bug you want to avoid! The **most venomous centipede** is known for being fast and aggressive – two qualities that make it extra dangerous... It latches on to a victim with its legs, before puncturing the skin with its "forcipules" (pincers) and injecting venom. Bites are extremely painful, but very rarely fatal to humans.

PROFILE: BRETT HAASE & AHRANI LOGAN, *AugmentifyIt®* founders

How did *AugmentifyIt®* begin?
We wanted to create something that parents and teachers could easily use to help kids to explore Science, Technology, Engineering, Arts and Maths (STEAM) subjects in a new, fun way. Augmented reality was an exciting technology that had potential to make these areas more "real".

What makes amazing AR content?
Amazing content needs to both enhance users' experience and leave them wanting to engage even more. For us, it has to be realistic, relevant, educational and interactive.

How do you create an AR bug?
AR can be triggered through animations, 3D objects or even video. Once you've decided the form of the content, you need people who have the skill sets to create it. Brett is a software developer and is able to take that content and flesh out detail in colours, shading and movement by working with computer code. He then places the finished bug into the app and tests it – a *lot*.

What's the most impressive AR animal you've ever seen?
We've seen a few AR dinosaurs that have been pretty awesome – and scary!

GIANT ASIAN MANTIS

Praying mantids come in many shapes, sizes and colours, but with 3D vision, lightning-quick reflexes and expert camouflage, all are perfectly adapted for hunting other insects. The giant Asian mantis (see also pp.82–83) is one of the bigger members of the family – indeed, it's the **heaviest praying mantis**.

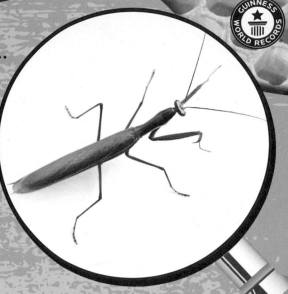

MONARCH BUTTERFLY

You probably think of butterflies as delicate, but there's nothing frail about this species. Once a year, monarchs embark on the **longest butterfly journey**, flying from Canada and the USA to the warmer climes of Mexico. One tagged individual in 1989 is estimated to have travelled 4,635 km (2,880 mi) – that's comparable to the flight between the US cities of New York and Los Angeles!

EMPEROR SCORPION

Also known as the imperial scorpion, this African arachnid can grow between 13 and 18 cm (5–7 in) long. Weighing some 60 g (2 oz) – about the same as a plum – it's the **heaviest scorpion**. Despite their formidable appearance, they're fairly harmless to humans, with their sting likened to that from a bee or wasp. In fact, some people keep them as pets!

How does a mother emperor scorpion carry her babies? a) In a sedan chair; b) On a leaf; c) On her back

ASIA

Comprising about 30% of all land on Earth, it's little wonder that the planet's largest **continent** is brimming with life...

Highest-living mammal
The rabbit-like large-eared pika lives on rocky slopes of the Himalayas and the Tibetan Plateau at dizzying heights of around 6,130 m (20,110 ft). They're sometimes called "whistling hares" owing to their high-pitched alarm calls.

16

8

9

13

14

6

10

16

4

15

3

1

11

7

2

5

16

17

12

See **Europe**, pp.68-69

Most aquatic crocodilian
17 Compared with other crocodile species, the slender-jawed gharial has weak legs, so the only way it can move on land is by sliding on its belly. As a result, it never strays far from rivers in India and Nepal. By contrast, in the water, it's a very quick and nimble swimmer.

Largest peafowl

India's blue peacocks are the most iconic member of this bird family, but they're not the biggest. That title goes to the green peacock, found notably on the Indonesian island of Java. With that show-stopping tail, a male can reach 3 m (9 ft 10 in) long.

Newest ape

Once believed to have been Sumatran orangutans, Tapanuli orangutans were officially recognized as a new species on 2 Nov 2017. Key traits that distinguish these close relatives include a smaller head and frizzier fur, as well as a slightly different diet.

Farthest head rotation by a mammal

No mammal's neck is more flexible than the tarsier's. These nocturnal primates from south-east Asia can turn their heads nearly 180° in each direction – giving them a total rotation of almost 360°! They also have the **largest eyes for a mammal (relative to body size)**.

Largest hammerhead shark

With their flattened heads and spaced-out eyes, hammerheads are one of the most unusual-looking creatures in the ocean! Of the nine known species, the biggest – by far – is the great hammerhead, which can attain lengths of 20 ft (6.1 m).

How many animals can you identify on this map? See pp.186–87 for answers.

Tyrannosaurus rex might be the most famous killer dino (see pp.100–01), but it wasn't the biggest. That title goes to the 9-tonne (19,840-lb) *Spinosaurus*: the **largest carnivorous dinosaur.** Estimated to have been 17 m (56 ft) from head to tail, this terrifying beast – from what is now North Africa – would have outsized the *T. rex* by as much as 4 m (13 ft)! However, the two apex predators would never have met as the *Spinosaurus* died out some 10 million years before *T. rex* roared on to the scene.

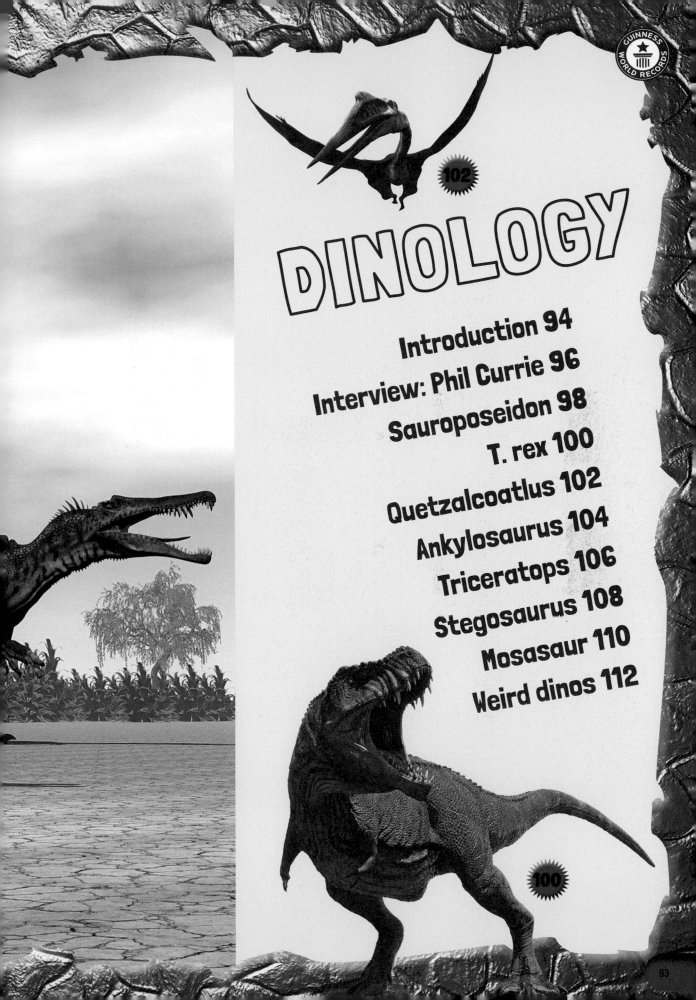

DINOLOGY

102

100

INTRODUCTION

If you exclude birds, dinosaurs haven't lived on Earth for more than 66 million years. But if the blockbuster *Jurassic Park* franchise – the **highest-grossing dino movie series** – has taught us anything, it's this: few animals in the history of our planet inspire more wonder and fascination than dinosaurs and their fellow prehistoric cousins.

Just as in the modern animal kingdom, some of these ancient creatures stood out from the crowd: they were record-breaking reptiles. This special chapter is a celebration of those superlative beasts of the Triassic, Jurassic and Cretaceous eras.

Discover which were the largest dinosaurs, which had the most powerful bite and which had the smallest brains – plus also get acquainted with a few of the more unusual family members!

WHAT IS A DINOSAUR?

Despite what we're often told, scientifically speaking all true dinosaurs were land-based. They fell into two groups based on the shape of their hip bones. Saurischians, such as *T. rex*, were "reptile-hipped", while Ornithischians – such as the *Tenontosaurus* below – were "bird-hipped".

Prehistoric oceans were brimming with many different marine reptiles. These included the ichthyosaurs (example below), plesiosaurs and mosasaurs. Unlike dinos, they were adapted for an aquatic lifestyle, with streamlined bodies, flippers and fish-like tails.

Although descended from the same ancestor as dinosaurs and closely related, pterosaurs were their own group. These flying reptiles were characterized by long beaks and large membranous wings, which stretched between an elongated digit and their bodies.

Dinosaurs and their relations lived on our planet for around 185 million years, spanning the Mesozoic era. Their time on Earth is divided into three key periods: the Triassic, the Jurassic and the Cretaceous. On the features in this chapter, we have highlighted the period to which each species dates, indicating roughly how many million years ago (MYA) that dinosaur lived. We have followed the dating system set out by geological experts at the International Commission of Stratigraphy.

MESOZOIC								
TRIASSIC			JURASSIC			CRETACEOUS		
251.9–201.3 MYA			201.3–145 MYA			145–66 MYA		
EARLY	MIDDLE	LATE	EARLY	MIDDLE	LATE	EARLY	MIDDLE	LATE

TIMELINE

INTERVIEW
PHIL CURRIE

A palaeontologist, museum curator and university professor, world-famous dino hunter Phil proves just how inspirational breakfast-cereal freebies can be!

Who or what first got you interested in dinosaurs?

My introduction came about when I was six years old through plastic toys given away in boxes of Rice Krispies. I was a dinosaur fanatic from that point forward. Aged 11, I read *All About Dinosaurs* by Roy Chapman Andrews. It was really a book about what it was like to be a dinosaur palaeontologist, and the day I read it, I decided that's what I'd be.

Why are dinosaurs so popular?

As children, I think our fascination focuses on the fact they were the biggest, tallest, heaviest, meanest, most ferocious... and all of those other superlatives. But as we get older, we're more interested in the mysteries, such as why did most dinosaurs disappear some 65 million years ago, after they had dominated the ecosystems on land for almost 150 million years?

Is there scope for us to bring back a dinosaur? And *should* we?

I used to think it'd be impossible, but considering the technological advances of the last 20 years, now I'm not so sure. If we ever figured out how to do it, though, I'd be 100% in favour of going ahead – under highly controlled conditions, of course!

Do you have your own personal collection of fossils?

When I was young, I was an avid fossil collector. Once I became a professional palaeontologist, though, I gave almost all of my collection to a university. I kept just a handful of specimens that were important for the stories I could tell about them.

What was it like to be part of the "greatest-ever expedition", the Canada–China Dinosaur Project?

It was an amazing experience, and changed me forever in subtle ways. We worked on known fossil sites in both countries, as well as discovering new ones – and collected more than 60 tonnes [132,300 lb] of fossils in China alone. It was a huge success. Professional relationships we developed then are still going strong.

What's the most exciting dig you've ever been on?

Perhaps the most exhilarating of all was when we collected *Cryolophosaurus*, not far from the South Pole. We were almost 4,000 m [13,120 ft] above sea level, high on Mt Kirkpatrick [see photo opposite]. The conditions were extreme, the scenery was beautiful and the expedition was a huge success!

Phil (right) and Rodolfo Coria next to a reconstruction of a *Mapusaurus* skull. The pair described and named the dino in 2006.

How do we work out what a dinosaur may have looked like from just a few bones?

The more that we know about a particular group of dinosaurs, the easier it is to work out what an individual may have looked like. A single tyrannosaur tooth is all I need to interpret the size and appearance of the animal. But we still have our mysteries. A pair of arms collected by a Polish–Mongolian expedition in 1965 led to many decades of speculation about what *Deinocheirus* looked like. When we finally found more complete

PALAEONTOLOGY PARADISE

Phil was involved in setting up the Royal Tyrrell Museum in Alberta, Canada, which is located in one of the richest dinosaur areas in the world. It focuses on local finds, and specializes in fossil preservation, research and display, spreading the word through school and public programmes and science camps.

ROYAL TYRRELL MUSEUM

NAME THAT DINO!

Mini meat-eater *Hesperonychus* ("western claw") was probably less than 1 m (3 ft 3 in) long. Phil helped to describe it in 2009.

Co-naming the anteater-like *Albertonykus borealis*, Phil explained that it probably ate termites, using its forelimbs to tear into logs.

Described by Phil and Yoichi Azuma, *Fukuiraptor* from Japan was later found to be not a raptor but a type of theropod.

skeletons in the Gobi Desert in 2009 and 2010, we were amazed by how bizarre the animal really was [see p.112]!

How have techniques evolved over the course of your career?

In some ways, things have hardly changed at all in 150 years – we still do a lot of physical labour and use plaster and burlap [coarse material made from plant fibres] to collect skeletons, for example. But now we have tools to help us do our job better, including drones, GPS technology, portable X-ray machines and scanning electron microscopes. It's hard to believe that many of our recent discoveries about the largest reptiles that ever lived have been made on a microscopic scale!

Any advice to readers considering a career in palaeontology?

People often think that we know almost everything there is to know about dinosaurs because we've been working on their fossils for nearly 200 years. But I doubt that we know even 1% of 1% of the dinosaur species that existed. There are many thousands that still need to be discovered.

When I started, there were probably fewer than half a dozen people in the world who were paid to research dinosaurs.

Phil and his wife, Eva Koppelhus, in Antarctica in 2010. Mt Kirkpatrick, where *Cryolophosaurus* was collected, appears in the background.

Four decades later, there are 20 times the number of research jobs – and the field is still growing.

Tell us about any record-breaking finds you've been involved with.

When we were working in China, we were collecting a sauropod dinosaur in Xinjiang in the north-west of the country. A rib that I was working on was over 3 m [9 ft 10 in] long, but since that was a bigger project than I wanted at the time, I moved on to another quarry where we collected the original *Sinraptor dongi*.

The big-ribbed sauropod – later called *Mamenchisaurus sinocanadorum* – took two more years to collect, and was for many years the largest sauropod known from Asia.

Another biggie was the discovery in 1997 of what we thought was a single skeleton of *Giganotosaurus* in Argentina. After four years of excavations, we had parts of nine skeletons of what we would later call *Mapusaurus roseae* – it was one of the largest meat-eating dinosaurs ever.

Being a palaeontologist totally rocks!

Phil takes a "laid back" approach to collecting a skull of the hadrosaur *Saurolophus* in Mongolia in 2010.

SAUROPOSEIDON

Meat-eaters such as the tyrannosaurs and velociraptors often steal the show in dinosaur movies and documentaries, but vegetarian sauropods were the true giants of the prehistoric age. The supersized family boasted many record-breakers, including *Diplodocus*, which had the **longest tail on a dinosaur**, stretching up to 14 m (45 ft).

The *Sauroposeidon* was a giant among giants. It's thought to be the **tallest dinosaur** ever to walk the Earth; today, it would comfortably be able to look into a skyscraper's sixth-floor window! Its height was mainly provided by its elongated neck – the **longest neck on a dinosaur**.

Each neck bone was up to 1.4 m (4 ft 7 in) and filled with pockets of air to keep it light. The neck alone is estimated to have measured 11-12 m (36-39 ft)

Relatively short legs meant its speed was likely limited to under 5 mph (8 km/h)

METRES

Although Sauroposeidon was the **tallest dinosaur**, it wasn't the **heaviest**. That title goes to one of its relations, the titanosaur *Argentinosaurus*. This Late Cretaceous giant weighed 60–124 tonnes (132,277–273,373 lb)!

SAUROPOSEIDON

SCIENTIFIC NAME: *Sauroposeidon proteles*

LENGTH: Up to 34 m (111 ft)

HEIGHT: Up to 18 m (59 ft)

WEIGHT: Up to 60 tonnes (132,277 lb)

DIET: Herbivore, e.g., leaves, flowers

FOSSILS DISCOVERED: 1994

RANGE: North America

Owing to the stress that holding up its huge neck would have put on its heart, Sauroposeidon mostly kept its head low, parallel to the ground

Impressions of sauropod skin suggest it was comprised of lots of small, knobbly scales, aka "tubercles"

TIMELINE	TRIASSIC			JURASSIC			CRETACEOUS		
	251.9–201.3 MYA			201.3–145 MYA			145–66 MYA		
	EARLY	MIDDLE	LATE	EARLY	MIDDLE	LATE	EARLY	MIDDLE	LATE

T. REX

With its name translating as "king of the tyrant lizards", *Tyrannosaurus rex* is widely considered the de facto dinosaur. Thanks to its ferocious reputation and countless appearances in blockbusters such as *Jurassic Park*, it's the first species that pops into many of our heads on hearing the word "dinosaur". The voracious carnivore lived in forests and river plains, chowing down on other huge dinos, with the **strongest land animal bite ever**. The powerful jaws generated about as much force as a medium-size elephant sitting on you! *T. rex* lived in the dinosaurs' final heyday, until their extinction some 66 million years ago.

T. rex stood roughly 12 ft (3.7 m) at the hip - about as tall as an African elephant. When rearing, its head could be 15-20 ft (4.6-6.1 m) off the ground

Scientists now believe that T. rex had bumpy, scaled skin - not feathers like some other dinosaurs

METRES

6
4
2

2   4   6   8   10   12   14

Eyeballs were around the size of tennis balls

Serrated, knife-like teeth were about the same size as the spine of this book!

T. REX

SCIENTIFIC NAME: *Tyrannosaurus rex*

LENGTH: Up to 13 m (42 ft)

WEIGHT: Up to 8.1 tonnes (9 US tons)

DIET: Carnivore, e.g., *Triceratops*, hadrosaurs, *T. rex*

FOSSILS DISCOVERED: 1902

RANGE: North America

T. rex's infamously "short" arms were actually about 1 m (3 ft 3 in) long and tipped with two taloned digits

The **most complete T. rex skeleton** – named "Sue" – sold in 1997 for $8.3 m (£5.1 m) to the Field Museum in Chicago, Illinois, USA. Sue's are the **most expensive dinosaur bones** sold to date.

TIMELINE	TRIASSIC			JURASSIC			CRETACEOUS		
	251.9–201.3 MYA			201.3–145 MYA			145–66 MYA		
	EARLY	MIDDLE	LATE	EARLY	MIDDLE	LATE	EARLY	MIDDLE	LATE

QUETZALCOATLUS

It's not a bird. It's not a plane. And it's not technically a dinosaur either... But this enormous reptile – with a wingspan greater than an F-16 fighter jet – was the **largest flying creature ever** to live on Earth.

The *Quetzalcoatlus* soared in the skies of the Late Cretaceous and was named after an Aztec feathered serpent god. Most of its remains have been found far inland, suggesting that it may have been a stalker of small vertebrates, rather like a modern-day stork.

The winged giant was also the **largest pterosaur**, standing as tall as a giraffe on the ground. This order of reptiles is believed to have been the first animals – after insects – to have evolved to fly.

Like all pterosaurs, it had wings made of thin, possibly hairy, skin, which were suited to gliding on updrafts

QUETZALCOATLUS

SCIENTIFIC NAME: *Quetzalcoatlus northropi*

HEIGHT: Up to 5.5 m (18 ft)

WEIGHT: 200–250 kg (440–550 lb)

WINGSPAN: 11–13 m (36–42 ft)

DIET: Carnivore, e.g., reptiles, carrion

FOSSILS DISCOVERED: 1971

RANGE: North America

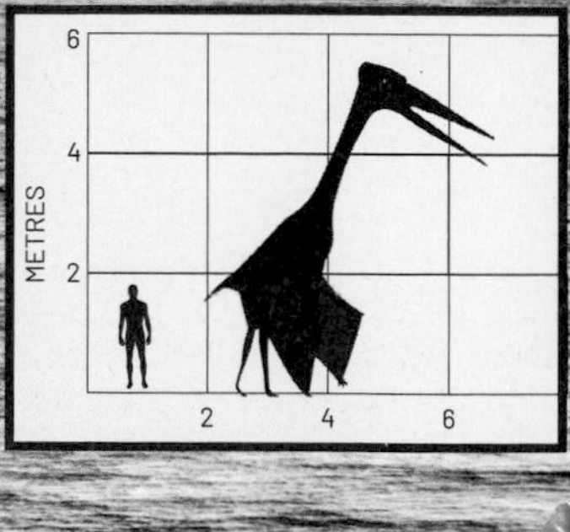

TIMELINE	TRIASSIC			JURASSIC			CRETACEOUS		
	251.9–201.3 MYA			201.3–145 MYA			145–66 MYA		
	EARLY	MIDDLE	LATE	EARLY	MIDDLE	LATE	EARLY	MIDDLE	LATE

Large eye sockets suggest that it had good eyesight, so could scan the ground for prey from the sky

Three claws on the front edge of each wing were used for grabbing on to live prey

The elongated neck could have been used to pluck up animals from the ground, a bit like some storks do today

The sharp, toothless beak was longer than an adult man is tall!

Scientists think that Quetzalcoatlus would have been too heavy to take off by flapping its wings. Instead, it may have used a similar technique to today's albatrosses – the **largest-winged living birds** – by running downhill or launching off a high cliff.

ANKYLOSAURUS

·If you were a herbivore in a land of massive meat-eaters such as *T. rex*, it paid to have a defence strategy or two up your sleeve. The **largest armoured dinosaur**, *Ankylosaurus*, took self-preservation to a whole new level. Probably about as tall as a horse, this 4-tonne (8,818-lb) plant-eater measured as much as 2.5 m (8 ft) across, making it also the **widest dinosaur (relative to length)**. Its chunky body – more than a mouthful for even the biggest jaws – was shielded by bony plates and an arsenal of hard, pointed peaks. Not to mention that famous wrecking ball of a tail...!

The tail club, made of tightly interlocking vertebrae and finished with a large bony ball, could swing freely from side to side. This weapon could hit hard enough to crush bone!

Broad and heavy, with a low centre of gravity, these sturdy beasts were very hard to topple over

TIMELINE	TRIASSIC			JURASSIC			CRETACEOUS		
	251.9–201.3 MYA			201.3–145 MYA			145–66 MYA		
	EARLY	MIDDLE	LATE	EARLY	MIDDLE	LATE	EARLY	MIDDLE	LATE

Bones in the dinosaur's skull and other parts of its body were fused together, increasing their strength and making them practically bite-proof. This feature is the source of the genus name, "fused lizard".

The bony plates - "scutes" - covering the dinosaur's back were similar to those sported by crocodiles and armadillos today

ANKYLOSAURUS

SCIENTIFIC NAME: *Ankylosaurus magniventris*

LENGTH: 7.5–10.7 m (24 ft 7 in–35 ft 1 in)

HEIGHT (at hips): 1.7 m (5 ft 6 in)

DIET: Herbivore, e.g., ferns, grass, leaves

RANGE: North America

FOSSILS DISCOVERED: 1906

One downside of a super-thick skull is that it doesn't leave much space for a brain! It's thought that Ankylosaurus had a great sense of smell, though, so could sniff out food and predators without having to think too hard

Solidly shielded from the top, the Ankylosaurus had little or no protection on its underside. Its most vulnerable area was its naked belly

TRICERATOPS

It's apt that the most famous feature of the "three-horned face" dino is also what secures its place in the record books. With up to 4-ft-long (1.2-m) horns – outdoing those of today's rhinos – *Triceratops* had the **longest dinosaur horns**. It shares this record with its horned relatives *Torosaurus* and *Coahuilaceratops*.

There's some debate around what this school-bus-sized plant-eater used its pointy headgear for. Some scientists say that the horns were used primarily for self-defence, warding off attacks by the likes of *T. rex*. Others think that they served more like a deer's antlers, used by males to resolve disputes during the mating season. It's possible that they may have been used for both, and perhaps for other roles besides.

The ceratopsids ("horn-faced dinosaurs") were one of the most diverse dino families. Although they all share horns, a frill and a beak, the size, shape and colour of these features varied dramatically between species (see p.112).

Sturdy elephant-like legs terminated in multiple hooves (three on each front foot and four on each back foot)

Two massive brow horns sat above the eyes, while the third horn, on the snout, was much stubbier

A bony frill may have been used for protecting the neck and for communication with other Triceratops

TRICERATOPS

SCIENTIFIC NAME: *Triceratops horridus*

LENGTH: Up to 9 m (29 ft)

WEIGHT: Up to 14 tonnes (30,864 lb)

DIET: Herbivore, e.g., leaves, palms, ferns

FOSSILS DISCOVERED: 1887

RANGE: North America

The ceratopsids had the largest dinosaur skulls. Their heads alone could be in excess of 3 m (9 ft 10 in) from front to back, including the bony frill

A hooked beak - like a turtle's - was used to tear off tough leaves. It then chewed them with as many as 800 teeth!

	METRES				
4					
2					
		2	4	6	8	10

TIMELINE	TRIASSIC			JURASSIC			CRETACEOUS		
	251.9–201.3 MYA			201.3–145 MYA			145–66 MYA		
	EARLY	MIDDLE	LATE	EARLY	MIDDLE	LATE	EARLY	MIDDLE	LATE

MOSASAUR

While dinosaurs ruled over the land, Earth's oceans boasted their very own prehistoric giants, perfectly adapted for aquatic life. None were bigger than the mosasaurs, the top predators of the Cretaceous sea.

There's some debate over just how long these marine reptiles may have reached. *Hainosaurus bernardi* has been estimated at 15 m (49 ft), or more conservatively at 12 m (39 ft). While *Mosasaurus hoffmanni* may have been as long as 18 m (59 ft) from head to tail – that's almost the length of a bowling alley!

While the specific figures are contested, one thing's for sure: mosasaurs are the **largest lizards ever** to live on Earth.

A long, streamlined body helped to reduce drag, allowing a mosasaur to cut through the water at speed, like today's sharks and dolphins

A flattened, shark-like tail was this predator's primary means of propulsion

METRES
2

Mosasaurs had four flippers, which were used mainly for steering

MOSASAURUS

SCIENTIFIC NAME: *Mosasaurus hoffmanni*

LENGTH: 17–18 m (55–59 ft)

WEIGHT: 15–20 tonnes (33,100–44,100 lb)

DIET: Carnivore, e.g., fish, ammonites, turtles

FOSSILS DISCOVERED: 1764

RANGE: North America, Europe, Atlantic Ocean

Eyes were positioned to the sides of the head for a more aerodynamic profile. This would have resulted in poor depth perception, though

Cone-shaped teeth were designed for gripping on to slippery prey, rather than cutting

A double-hinged jaw and flexible skull provided a massive gape, allowing mosasaurs to swallow large animals whole

Tiny, oval-shaped scales, each with a central ridge, covered the body, helping these marine giants to glide through the water

Genetically speaking, monitor lizards are some of the closest descendants of mosasaurs today. The family includes the world's **largest lizard**, the Komodo dragon (see pp.134–35).

TIMELINE	TRIASSIC			JURASSIC			CRETACEOUS		
	251.9–201.3 MYA			201.3–145 MYA			145–66 MYA		
	EARLY	MIDDLE	LATE	EARLY	MIDDLE	LATE	EARLY	MIDDLE	LATE

111

WEIRD DINOS

Palaeontologists have been studying dinosaur remains for almost 200 years. But since the only evidence they have to go on is incredibly ancient and fragmented, a great deal of what we think we know about these creatures is based on educated guesswork. Nevertheless, scientists have now named nearly a thousand different species. Many of them had extraordinary characteristics, but some – like the multi-horned *Kosmoceratops* with its bony comb-over and the mini *Microraptor* with its four wings – stand out for their sheer oddity...

DEINOCHEIRUS

Named for its "unusual terrible hands", the **bipedal dinosaur with the longest arms** had three huge claws on each 2.4-m (7-ft 10-in) arm. Beaked and humpbacked, this ostrich-like dinosaur seems to have been constructed from a pack of mismatched body parts!

KOSMOCERATOPS

With 10 horns and spikes on its frill, a horn above each eye, one on its nose and one on each cheek, the **most horned animal ever** went in for Late Cretaceous bling in a big way. Palaeontologists believe that the display was for attracting mates rather than defence, unlike the *Triceratops* (see pp.106–07).

OMG!

The **largest dinosaur footprints** – found in Australia in 2017 – are as long as a man is tall!

112

MICRORAPTOR

The **smallest dinosaur** was the feathered *Microraptor zhaoianus*, which would be dwarfed by a domestic cat at just 39 cm (15.3 in) long. Over 60% of its body length was tail! A fossil of the dinky dino was found in China in 1999.

DID YOU KNOW?

Some dinosaurs, such as the giant "deceptive lizard" *Apatosaurus*, may have been able to create a sonic boom by whipping their tails!

AMARGASAURUS

All animals' vertebrae (even yours) have small raised bits known as "neural spines". But this sauropod, with the **longest neural spines**, took the bony mane to a new level! The function of the feature – some 60 cm (2 ft) high – isn't certain, but perhaps the rods could have been shaken together to make a rattling noise that signalled to other dinosaurs.

GIGANTORAPTOR

At 8 m (26 ft) long and 5 m (16 ft) tall, the **largest *Gigantoraptor* fossil** was certainly gigantic, but the dinosaur it belonged to wasn't a raptor – it was an "oviraptorosaur". Longer and taller than an African elephant, most of this dino's bulk was in the torso. The spindly arms, meanwhile, look as though they have been borrowed from a much skinnier cousin!

165

Millions of years that dinosaurs lived on Earth. Modern humans have managed only about 300,000 years so far...

AUSTRALASIA

Having been isolated for millions of years, the smallest continent has more than its fair share of unusual creatures!

Heaviest brain

1 The sperm whale's 9-kg (19-lb 13-oz) brain accounts for just 0.02% of the animal's total weight, but is still six times heavier than a human's! Also the **largest toothed mammal**, the sperm whale is among 45 or so cetaceans that call Australian waters their home.

Sleepiest marsupial

10 The koala eats almost nothing but high-fibre, low-nutrition eucalyptus leaves – then spends 18 hr out of every 24 sleeping while it digests them! (For more of nature's sleepyheads, see pp.42–43.) Mother koalas teach their joeys to eat different types of eucalyptus leaves to balance their diet.

Heaviest reptile

13 One of the most feared animals down under, saltwater crocodiles live in estuaries and billabong lakes throughout northern Australia. "Salties" can swallow prey such as pigs and even buffalo whole. No wonder they can weigh 1,200 kg (2,645 lb)!

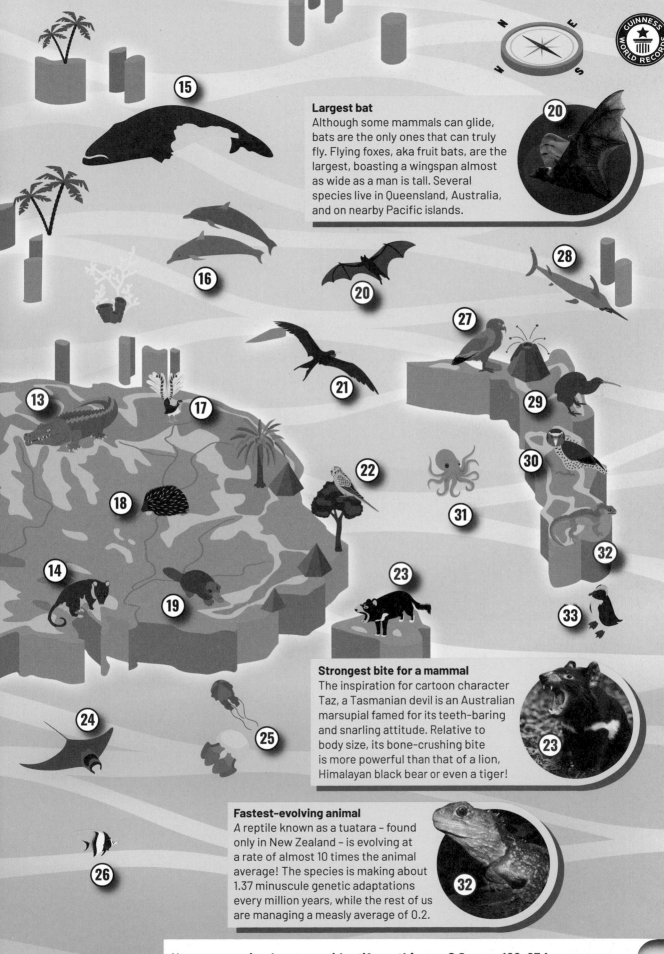

Largest bat
Although some mammals can glide, bats are the only ones that can truly fly. Flying foxes, aka fruit bats, are the largest, boasting a wingspan almost as wide as a man is tall. Several species live in Queensland, Australia, and on nearby Pacific islands.

Strongest bite for a mammal
The inspiration for cartoon character Taz, a Tasmanian devil is an Australian marsupial famed for its teeth-baring and snarling attitude. Relative to body size, its bone-crushing bite is more powerful than that of a lion, Himalayan black bear or even a tiger!

Fastest-evolving animal
A reptile known as a tuatara – found only in New Zealand – is evolving at a rate of almost 10 times the animal average! The species is making about 1.37 minuscule genetic adaptations every million years, while the rest of us are managing a measly average of 0.2.

How many animals can you identify on this map? See pp.186–87 for answers.

115

STAND-UP SERPENT

The deadly king cobra of south-east Asia and India is the **longest venomous snake**. One specimen found in Malaysia in 1937 grew to 5.7 m (18 ft 8 in). Cobras can raise up to a third of their bodies off the ground – bringing them eye-to-eye with a grown man – while still moving forward to attack. They expand the sides of their necks to form a menacing hood flare and some even spit venom just to be sure they get their message across!

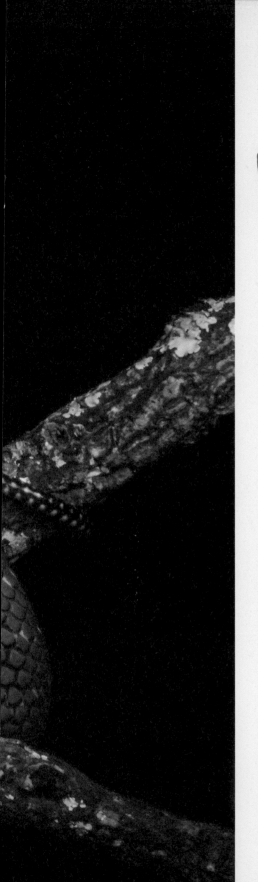

132

DANGER ZONE

122

THE REAL ANGRY BIRDS

Forget Red, Chuck, Bomb and the gang... You're about to meet the avian world's real-life bruisers!

A relative of ostriches and emus, the prehistoric-looking cassowary is regarded as the **most dangerous bird** on Earth.

They're instantly distinguished by their size (they stand about as tall as an 11-year-old boy), a bright blue face with two red flaps of skin ("wattles") dangling from their neck, and a horn-like helmet on their heads called a "casque".

But none of the above is what makes them so feared. For that, you have to look at their feet (right). On their inner toe, these birds sport a super-sharp claw that can be as long as 12 cm (5 in)! A kick with this spike can easily cause serious injury, or even death...

Cassowaries use their dagger-like claws not only as weapons, but also to forage and improve grip when running.

SOUTHERN CASSOWARY

SCIENTIFIC NAME: *Casuarius casuarius*

TYPE: Bird

HEIGHT: 1.5–2 m (4 ft 11 in–6 ft 6 in)

WEIGHT: Up to 60 kg (132 lb)

DIET: Omnivore, e.g., fruit, carrion, fungi, insects

LIFESPAN: 30 years

RANGE: Australia and New Guinea

MORE BEASTLY BIRDS...

Swooping magpies terrorize Australians every spring. In 2017 alone, there were over 3,000 magpie-related attacks.

Northern goshawks are infamous for their fearless aerial raids. They target the heads of not only humans but also horses, wolves and even bears!

Visitors to British seaside resorts are often dive-bombed by "hangry" gulls. Some people have been left bleeding after these seabirds strike.

I wish these chicks would hurry up and hatch – I'm dying for a pee!

It's pretty hard to miss a cassowary's eggs... The shells are bright green and they measure about three times as big as a chicken's egg! Females lay a clutch (typically four or five eggs) in a shady spot, surrounded by a ring of scraped-up leaf litter, earth and grass.

Once the eggs are laid, the males take over. Incubating them for up to two months, they barely leave the nest other than for a quick drink. After the babies hatch, dad raises the kids, teaching them what to eat and protecting them for around nine months. The stripy, brown chicks (above) look very different from the brightly coloured adults to help camouflage them on the sun-dappled forest floor.

Cassowaries spend most of their lives in the tropical rainforest. However, as humans continue to encroach on their natural habitat, we're bumping into these giant birds in unexpected places more and more. Sightings now occur on forest roads, banana plantations and even on busy beaches! The most common coastal areas to see them is where the forest runs down to the shore, with hotspots including Mission Beach and Moresby Range (left) – both on Australia's north-eastern coast.

Cassowaries are now such a common sight on some beaches in Australia that locals barely even bat an eyelid!

92
Years since a human was killed by a cassowary. The victim, Phillip McClean, tripped while hunting the bird.

The southern cassowary is the second-heaviest bird in the world, beaten only by the... a) Emu; b) Ostrich; c) Golden eagle

ANOPHELES MOSQUITO

SCIENTIFIC NAME: *Anopheles*

TYPE: Insect

WINGSPAN: 2.8–4.4 mm (0.11–0.17 in)

WEIGHT: 2.5 mg (0.00008 oz)

DIET: Omnivore, e.g., blood, nectar, algae

LIFESPAN: 1–2 weeks

RANGE: Worldwide

50 M

The distance from which a mosquito can detect us via the carbon dioxide that we produce (164 ft).

THE MINI MASS MURDERER

You'd probably think that the world's **deadliest animals** are big, scary beasts with lots of teeth, right? In reality, the worst culprits, responsible for billions of deaths, are no larger than your fingernail.

Tiny female *Anopheles* mosquitoes (males are vegetarian) can have even tinier disease-causing parasites, called *Plasmodium*, living inside them. When mosquitoes slurp a few drops of our blood, some of these parasites get transferred to our bodies. This can lead to life-threatening conditions such as malaria.

It's estimated that mosquitoes are to blame for as many as 725,000–1 million deaths per year. That's up to 20 times more than the annual victims of crocodiles, sharks and snakes combined!

BIG PICTURE

A mosquito with a full belly of blood can measure up to three times its pre-meal weight!

MOSQUITOES IN MINIATURE

Mosquitoes are occasionally targeted by parasitic bugs of their own, so in a strange twist of nature, the blood-sucker becomes the blood donor! Tiny *Culicoides* midges – which are only about 1 mm (0.04 in) long – have been observed feasting on the blood from abdomens of engorged mosquitoes (right). They also feed on cattle, dogs, birds and people.

Drinking which beverage increases the odds of being bitten by a mosquito? a) Beer; b) Milk; c) Orange juice

SWIMMERS, BEWARE!

Most of the time, there's little to beat a dip in the river or a snorkel in the sea – but sometimes you might want to think twice before you dive in!

1

3

4

2

5

9.9 TONNES
Food consumed per year (21,825 lb)

40 KM/H
Top speed achieved in short bursts (25 mph)

314
Unprovoked attacks on humans recorded since 1580. Of these, only 80 were fatal

300 TEETH
One mouthful, arranged in several rows

70 YEARS
Age a great white can reach

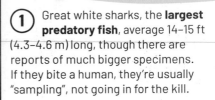

GUINNESS WORLD RECORDS

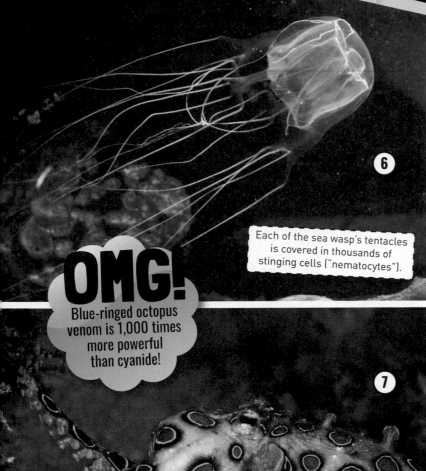

6

Each of the sea wasp's tentacles is covered in thousands of stinging cells ("nematocytes").

OMG!
Blue-ringed octopus venom is 1,000 times more powerful than cyanide!

7

① Great white sharks, the **largest predatory fish**, average 14–15 ft (4.3–4.6 m) long, though there are reports of much bigger specimens. If they bite a human, they're usually "sampling", not going in for the kill.

② Despite their scary reputation, piranhas (long deemed the **most ferocious freshwater fish**) are more likely to dine on fish, bugs or even fruit. They may nibble on carcasses but rarely attack people.

③ The **largest gulper eels** are a 2-m-long (6-ft 6-in) species known as "swallowers". Their mouths, with pouch-like lower jaws, open so wide that they can chow down on victims larger than they are!

④ Stonefish, from tropical Indo-Pacific waters, are masters of camouflage, blending in perfectly among coral. The **most venomous fish**, they have venom-filled sacs on each of the 13 spines on their backs.

⑤ With a head of about 2 cm (0.8 in) and teeth just over half that length, the Sloane's viperfish has the **largest teeth relative to head size for a fish**. It can impale prey just by swimming straight at it!

⑥ The Flecker's sea wasp, the **most venomous jellyfish**, is found in Indo-Pacific waters. This box jellyfish's potent venom – which attacks the heart, nervous system and skin – has killed dozens of people.

⑦ The toxic bite of the blue-ringed octopus can kill in a matter of minutes. Luckily, the **most venomous mollusc** tends to bite only when it's provoked!

Which of these are not predators of piranhas? a) Caiman; b) River dolphins; c) Capybaras

DANGER ZONE

INTERVIEW
STEVE BACKSHALL

Explorer, animal activist and *Deadly 60* host Steve is on a mission to convince the world that every species deserves our respect – especially the misrepresented "scary" ones!

Of all the dangerous and deadly animals you've met, which has most surprised you?
Deadly and dangerous aren't the same thing. If we just made programmes about animals that were dangerous to us as humans, they'd pretty much all be about mosquitoes [see pp.120–21]! Sharks, crocs, big cats and other obvious predators are very rarely dangerous to us, but the ways they've adapted to be deadly in *their* world – to their own prey – is what I find exciting.

Which of your animal encounters have been the most terrifying?
Very few animal encounters are terrifying – people are far more frightening than animals ever are. I've felt safer and more serene swimming in the sea alongside a great white shark than I ever do walking through a big city at night!

How do you prepare to go into potentially deadly wildlife territory?
It depends on the environment. The skills you need to

survive in Arctic or high-altitude conditions are different from those you need in deserts or jungles. It's all about experience and training, and knowing what's likely to be required in each different habitat.

You often work in extreme and inhospitable environments. Have you ever reached your limit?
I trained to be an expedition leader with the Indian Army in the high Himalayas. After five weeks of breaking a trail through thick snow, at high altitude and on low rations, I was wasting away. I lost 15% of my body weight and got quite weak. That's probably the closest I've come.

Have you got many expeditions planned for 2018?
I think I have 11 major expeditions in the diary – which will make it my biggest year yet. I'll barely be at home or in the UK at all.

Are there any non-predatory animals that fascinate you?
To a naturalist, all animals are fascinating. When I'm home, I quite happily watch the local songbirds, moths and butterflies. All wild things are inherently exciting to me.

Steve's awards include two BAFTAs from the British Academy of Film and Television Arts: Best Children's Television Presenter and Best Factual Series – both for *Deadly 60* (BBC, UK).

Do you think some predators get a reputation they don't deserve?
They *all* get reputations they don't deserve! Sharks kill fewer than 10 people a year worldwide, which is

STEVE BITES BACK!

Among other organizations, Steve works with Bite-Back, a UK charity dedicated to conserving sea life – particularly sharks. By persuading retailers to "put conservation before commerce", it champions species such as the great white (the **largest predatory fish**, left), rays, marlin and sawfish (right).

124

WHY SHARKS ARE AWESOME...

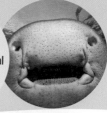

"They have electrosensitive organs in their snouts that can pick up electrical fields created by the moving muscles of their prey."

"There are over 400 species, of all different shapes and sizes. Many of these are small catsharks (aka dogfish), such as the small-spotted catshark [right], a nocturnal predator."

"The light-coloured 'lateral line' on a shark's side is made up of a series of pores. Super-sensitive, the line can detect prey from the tiniest of movements."

Steve takes the plunge armed only with a camera, demonstrating again that sharks' fearsome reputation is (usually!) undeserved.

all of which aim to change people's perception of sharks, and change the legislation that fails to protect them from humans. It's essential we tackle both, or we'll lose these beautiful animals completely.

Why do you think that sharks in particular are vilified and feared?
It's not too surprising: they're big fish with sharp teeth, and they live in an environment where we automatically feel vulnerable and exposed. And the media don't help!

What should you do if you encounter a shark in the wild?
Enjoy the experience! Keep a strong, confident body position, and don't thrash around or panic.

Any tips for people who want to work with dangerous animals?
Jump in and do it! It's such a rewarding, exciting way to make a living. Plus, the people who love animals are the very ones who are going to work out how to save them.

substantially fewer people than are killed just taking selfies! But a shark attack makes such a shocking story that when the press get hold of it, it soon becomes headline news.

Have you noticed differences in the ways that different countries and cultures respond to species?
Definitely! Many of the people I visit live with crocodiles at the bottom of their gardens, or venomous snakes in their attics. They know the real dangers and challenges involved, and are much more realistic about how to live and work around those animals.

How do you go about changing people's perceptions?
I must have engaged with several hundred-thousand people by now in my tours around the world. I talk about the wonder of sharks, and the rules for staying safe in shark seas – but my programmes always include a strong conservation message.

Tell us about your role as patron of the Shark Trust.
I work with the Shark Trust, Manta Trust and Bite-Back marine charities,

In which of the following areas is Steve also an expert? a) Martial arts; b) Hungry Hungry Hippos; c) Growing rare orchids

REAL-LIFE VAMPIRES

Unlike Count Dracula and his kin, blood-drinking animals – aka "sanguinivores" – aren't a thing of fiction. No cross or garlic is going to save you from these guys!

As they suck blood, leeches release an anaesthetic on to the wound, so their host may not immediately notice what's going on. They also use an anti-clotting chemical so that the blood keeps on flowing. The **largest leech** – the giant Amazon leech – can grow longer than this book when open... *Eek!*

MOST COMMON MUSK DEER

Siberian musk deer aren't actually bloodsuckers, but earn their place thanks to their vampirish fangs. The deer are herbivores, feeding on lichens, pine needles, leaves and tree bark. Males grow their tusk-like teeth – rather than antlers – to fight rivals.

The deep-sea-dwelling vampire squid isn't technically a vampire or a squid. It's actually something of a unique hybrid between a squid and an octopus. What is for sure is that this creature has the **largest eye-to-body ratio** of any animal, with 2.5-cm (0.9-in) peepers and a 28-cm-long (11-in) body.

FEWEST TEETH FOR A BAT

Some bats have as many as 38 teeth, but common vampire bats from Latin America have only 20. But they put them to good use: the upper incisors lack enamel, which keeps them razor-sharp. Vampire bats use them to inflict deep cuts on victims such as cows, then lap up the blood. They're the only mammals known to feed entirely on blood, but rarely attack humans.

3
SPECIES
The common vampire bat, the white-winged vampire bat and the hairy-legged vampire bat

100
BATS
Typical size of a vampire bat colony

20 g
Blood consumed by a female in a 20-min meal (0.7 oz). That's about a tablespoon

25
Cows' worth of blood that a 100-bat colony can consume in a year

10,000 x
Size difference between a vampire bat and its largest prey (e.g., cattle and horses)

OMG!
Leeches are still used in medicine to fight blood clots and restore blood flow.

LARGEST CARNIVOROUS BAT

There are about a dozen bat species worldwide that enjoy a meat-based diet of small birds, amphibians, reptiles and mammals – including other bats. The largest is the flap-nosed spectral bat – or "false vampire". Native to southern Mexico, Central and South America, its wingspan can exceed 1 m (3 ft 3 in). It doesn't drink blood, though, like its smaller cousins (see opposite).

LARGEST TICK

Blood-sucking hard ticks look spider-like before a meal (left), but inflate to the size of a walnut when they're engorged with blood (below). They sometimes feed on a host for weeks at a time before they drop off to look for shelter.
These parasites have been doing what they do for a very long time: fossilized ticks have been found from the Cretaceous era – 145 to 66 million years ago!

So, I hear you think small brown birds are a pain in the bum...?

The vampire finch lives only on Wolf and Darwin islands in the Galápagos archipelago of Ecuador, and it's the **most bloodthirsty bird**. While it typically eats seeds and bugs, it will also peck seabirds and drink the blood that seeps from the wound. Sometimes a whole gang of vampire finches will stand in line waiting their turn!

Fleas can jump how many times their own body length to find their next host? a) 8 times; b) 50 times; c) 200 times

SSSUPER SNAKES

Slithering, hissing, biting things... You probably think you know all there is to know about snakes, right? But did you know that some serpents are hiding secret powers?

1

By forming an "S" shape and undulating their bodies, flying snakes have some control over the direction in which they glide.

Is that the time? I must fly!

3

4

2

At some 2.5 m (8 ft 2 in) long, black mambas are the second-longest venomous snakes, beaten only by the king cobra (see pp.116–17).

1.7 m
Average length of the small-scaled snake's body (5 ft 6 in)

0
Recorded human deaths to date

110 mg
Most venom yielded from a single specimen (0.003 oz) – the average dose is 44 mg (0.001 oz)

0.01 MG/KG
Amount of venom required to kill a human

45 MIN
Estimated time it would take for a bite to cause death

GUINNESS WORLD RECORDS

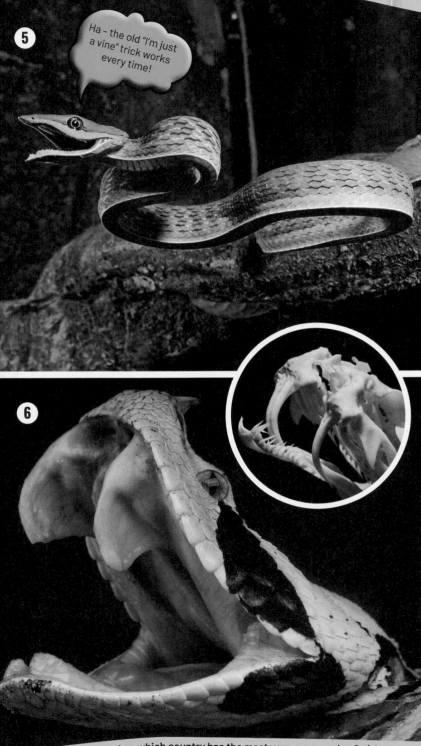

(5)

Ha – the old "I'm just a vine" trick works every time!

(6)

(1) Paradise flying snakes launch themselves off a branch, suck in their stomachs and flare their ribs to form a wing-like shape. They don't actually "fly" but can glide some 100 m (328 ft) between trees, making them the **most aerial snakes**.

(2) Black mambas – the **fastest snakes on land** – are the sprinters of serpent-kind. They can reach 16-19 km/h (10–12 mph) in short bursts over flat ground. Renowned for their aggressive nature, they're one of Africa's most feared animals.

(3) The eastern hognose is a master of deception. Whenever it senses danger, it goes belly-up and pretends to be dead. This survival tactic, also seen in opossums and insects, is known as "thanatosis".

(4) The venom of the small-scaled snake (aka the inland taipan) is about 50 times more toxic than that of the king cobra! The world's **most venomous snake** (see stats above) preys on rats and mice in the semi-desert of eastern central Australia.

(5) A green vine snake, aka flatbread snake, is so slender that it virtually disappears when viewed head-on. It spends most of its time in the trees, masquerading as foliage while hunting for birds.

(6) Not only are African Gaboon vipers extremely venomous, but they also have the **largest fangs for a snake**. Their terrifying teeth (shown more clearly in the inset of a skeleton) measure as long as 5 cm (2 in); that's about the same size as an adult's pinky finger. *Eek!*

With nine native species, which country has the most venomous snakes? a) Austria; b) Antigua; c) Australia

INTERVIEW
MARK O'SHEA

Serious doses of adventure and discovery keep this explorer, presenter, author and Professor of Herpetology focused on the world's most remarkable reptiles.

What first drew you to reptiles and amphibians?

I was drawn to reptiles – especially snakes – at an early age, perhaps because nobody else seemed to like them. The more I read about them, the more fascinated I became. We went on a family holiday to Ireland in the 1960s, and the reptile keeper at Dublin Zoo let me handle a huge boa constrictor, which was amazing.

Black caimans, such as Mark's shiny-eyed friend here, are the **largest caiman species** and can weigh in excess of 400 kg (881 lb).

What has been your most memorable expedition so far?

Spending seven months in the northern Amazon rainforest in 1987–88 was a real baptism of fire. I increased the known reptiles and amphibians of the region hugely during my stay... but that wasn't all! I survived my first rattlesnake bite, was thrown out of a somersaulting Land Cruiser and stung by a scorpion that I found in my hammock...

I'm particularly drawn to Papua New Guinea [PNG] and have worked with snakebite doctors from Oxford University there, collected venom for the Liverpool School of Tropical Medicine, and am now attached to the Australian Venom Research Unit, which is continuing the snake-bite research. I have been working on the snakes of New Guinea – the largest tropical island in the world – for many years and wrote the only field guide to its native snakes in 1996.

How do you find or track reptiles and amphibians in the wild?

You don't usually track reptiles as you would mammals, though I have caught vipers in the dunes of the Arabian Peninsula by following their markings in the sand at night. I once found three western diamondback rattlesnakes – "buzz tails" – in 10 min, outside Tucson, Arizona, by just listening for their rattling.

At night, you can use a torch to locate the eye-shine of frogs, crocodiles or caiman and South American tree boas, and you can road-cruise for snakes on tarmac after heavy rain. This works well in wetland or desert areas. Finding reptiles and amphibians usually means being patient: walking slowly and using your eyes and ears, stopping and looking around and investigating any rocks, rotten logs, tree holes, peeling bark or similar micro-habitats you find as you go along. You have to put the time and effort in to be successful.

Is it true that you were bitten by your own king cobra in 2012?

I did have a 10-ft (3-m) king cobra [see main picture]. She was called "Sleeping Beauty" because it once took me 100 hr to wake her from an anaesthetic! She lived at West Midland Safari Park, where I have been Curator of Reptiles for over 30 years. On one occasion she lunged while I was feeding her, but missed her lunch and bit my shoe instead. Because my venom-soaked sock then brushed against broken skin on my foot, I was envenomed. I was "medevaced" to hospital, but by the following day – by which time my

HOW VENOM WORKS

Different venoms act in different ways. Haemotoxins stop blood from clotting, so victims may bleed to death. Neurotoxins affect nerve messages, so can impact breathing. Cytotoxins dissolve tissue, and other venoms attack the heart or the kidneys. But some have been harnessed to save lives: not just as antivenoms but, for example, during heart surgery to prevent potentially fatal blood clots.

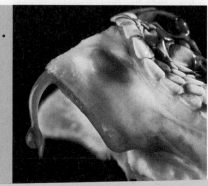

"Being with a live Komodo dragon, the **largest lizard**, is like stepping back thousands of years to when the **largest land lizard ever**, *Megalania*, roamed Australia."

"The king cobra – the **longest venomous snake** – is the only one that seems to have something going on behind the eyes. It looks to me as if it's thinking!"

"Alligator snapping turtles, the largest freshwater turtles of the Americas, are now protected. Thankfully populations are recovering."

"death" had already been reported in New Zealand and Australia! – I was well enough to be back at the Park.

I *was* bitten in 1993 by a large canebrake rattlesnake, but – 16 packs of antivenom and eight days later – I had fully recovered.

What's the best thing to do if you're bitten by a snake in the wilderness?

It depends on the type of snake and where in the world the bite happens. In Australia and PNG, the "Aussie Bandage", a pressure bandage, will slow down venom-absorption rates and give you time to get to hospital. Anything constrictive – e.g., rings or a watch – should be removed

Olive sea snakes such as this one on Ashmore Reef, off Australia, breathe air, but their entire life cycle occurs in the ocean.

from a bitten limb straight away. The DO NOTs are very important: no tourniquets, no razor-cutting the bite site, no alcohol or drugs, no ice-packs, no suction devices (they don't work) and no "traditional" techniques such as blackstones (they don't work either). At the very top of the list is: DO NOT waste time!

What advice can you offer aspiring herpetologists?

Never lose sight of your dream. I didn't follow a conventional route from school to university, having left school before my A-levels to work in a hospital. But I kept reading, asking questions and learning about

reptiles. Having then picked up an A-level in Zoology, I was offered a place as a mature student on a degree in Applied Sciences, and grabbed the chance with both hands. I went back into education and turned my hobby into my career. Now – among much else – I'm Professor of Herpetology at the University of Wolverhampton [in the West Midlands, UK].

You're never too old to learn. Several former work-experience assistants have now got zoo curatorial jobs or achieved PhDs. They realised their dreams by pushing themselves and believing they could do it.

Snakes and crocodiles don't come out at night if... a) There's a full Moon; b) It's Thursday; c) They've had a busy day

CUTE BUT DEADLY

Don't be fooled by the big eyes, bright colours and bundles of fluff – every one of these toxic critters could seriously endanger your health!

PUFFERFISH

Even edible fish have parts that are best avoided at dinner time. The **most poisonous edible fish** is the pufferfish of the Red Sea and Indo-Pacific region. Less than 0.1 g (0.004 oz) of the toxin stored in their spiky bodies can kill an adult – in just 20 min!

OMG!

A platypus detects prey via electrical impulses in its bill!

GILA MONSTER

Native to Mexico and south-western USA, the **most venomous lizard** has venom glands in its lower jaws and carries enough toxin to kill two people. Luckily, it usually attacks only when provoked!

GOLDEN POISON-DART FROG

Nobody calls me yellow and gets away with it!

The **most poisonous frog** contains enough toxin to kill 10 adult humans or 20,000 mice. The poison is called batrachotoxin, and even in the tiniest quantities can cause paralysis and death. This deadly little creature – only 4–5 cm (1.6–2 in) long – is also the **largest poison-dart frog**.

200 x

Strength of the killer Kermits' toxin compared to morphine

1 cm

Length of the smallest poison-dart frog species (0.4 in)

40
EGGS

Size of the largest poison-dart frog clutches

10
YEARS

Duration that the venom can stay active when it's coated on darts

0.002 mg

Amount of poison needed to kill a human

GUINNESS WORLD RECORDS

PLATYPUS

One of very few venomous mammals, the **lightest egg-laying mammal** delivers its poison via a sharp spur near its heels. The sting doesn't kill humans, but it can be fatal to smaller mammals such as dogs.

PYGMY SLOW LORIS

SCIENTIFIC NAME: *Nycticebus pygmaeus*

TYPE: Mammal

LENGTH: Up to 23 cm (9 in)

WEIGHT: 450 g (15.8 oz)

DIET: Omnivore, e.g., insects, fruit

LIFESPAN: 15 years

RANGE: South-east Asia and China

PYGMY SLOW LORIS

The **smallest species of loris**, the pygmy is native to Cambodia, China, Laos and Vietnam. It looks adorable with its big eyes, sweet smile and button nose – but stand back, as it secretes toxin from patches on its elbows. After licking, the chemicals transfer to its needle-sharp teeth, giving it a toxic bite. Couple that with a four-pawed iron grip, and the result isn't quite so cute!

HOODED PITOHUI

Native to Papua New Guinea, this innocent-looking songster is the **most poisonous bird**. Scientists accidentally discovered its poison in 1990 when preparing some of the species as museum exhibits. The pitohui's skin and feathers contain the same powerful toxin as that secreted by South American dart frogs (see opposite). We've yet to work out why, though...

Orange is the new black? Well, I've got both covered...

What are pufferfish known as in Japan, where they're considered a delicacy? a) Chow-chow; b) Gofo; c) Fugu

ALL ABOUT KOMODO DRAGONS

The largest lizard in the world today is a dragon with an awesome appetite: it has been known to double its body weight with a single meal!

With jaws lined with sharp serrated teeth, dagger-like curved claws and a super-long forked tongue, this monster reptile from Indonesia – the **largest lizard** – more than lives up to its fearsome name...

Scientists previously thought that bacteria lent Komodo dragons a toxic bite. However, in 2009, we discovered that their killer arsenal includes venom glands in the mouth. Able to secrete proteins that disable and infect their prey, this weapon makes these real-life dragons almost as deadly as their mythical, fire-breathing cousins!

KOMODO DRAGON

SCIENTIFIC NAME: *Varanus komodoensis*

TYPE: Reptile

LENGTH: 2.5 m (8 ft 6 in)

WEIGHT: 79–91 kg (175–200 lb)

DIET: Carnivore, e.g., deer, pigs, snakes, carrion

LIFESPAN: 30 years

RANGE: Lesser Sunda Islands, Indonesia

LEGS
It might have short, bowed legs, but the dragon can sprint at up to 20 km/h (12 mph) – although it prefers to hunt by stealth. Its "undulatory" walk, in which its head swings from side to side, helps it to sense and locate rotting flesh – sometimes from many miles away.

WHIP-LIKE TAIL
The dragon uses its tail for support when it stands on its back legs in a "tripod stance" to reach food or to fight. It's also useful for tripping or knocking over prey such as deer or buffalo.

Dragons can turn cannibal and sometimes dine on their own young. But babies have evolved a stinking good strategy to reduce their snack-appeal: they roll in dung!

US naturalist W Douglas Burden visited Komodo Island in the 1920s. The report of his trip inspired the 1933 movie *King Kong*.

Strong swimmers, dragons will sometimes paddle from one island to another in search of food.

CHAIN-MAIL SKIN

A dragon's rough, stone-coloured skin is reinforced with hardened scales called "osteoderms".

DEADLY BITE

Venom glands in the lower jaw release a toxic cocktail that causes paralysis and massive blood loss – so even if a bite doesn't kill, its effects soon will!

FORKED TONGUE

The tongue picks up tiny airborne taste particles, which dragons "test" inside their mouths to identify the nature – and location – of the source.

SICK TO THE STOMACH

If threatened, Komodos can throw up the contents of their stomachs to lighten the load before they make their escape!

WHERE IN THE WORLD?

KOMODO NATIONAL PARK

Located in the middle of the Indonesian archipelago between the islands of Sumbawa and Flores, Komodo National Park was founded in 1980 to protect Komodo dragons and their habitat. It now provides refuge for many other terrestrial animals, such as the orange-footed scrubfowl and thousands of marine species including fish, coral and sponges.

SINGLE-PARENT FAMILIES

Asexual reproduction, aka "parthenogenesis", is extremely rare in vertebrates, seen only in a handful of reptiles, fish and, on one occasion, a turkey! However, a Komodo dragon named Sungai at London Zoo – who hadn't been near a male for years – laid eggs that yielded live dragons in 2006. The babies were not clones of their mum, but did exclusively use her DNA. All four of Sungai's offspring grew up normally.

Komodo dragon eggs are roughly the size of... a) An orange; b) A grapefruit; c) A watermelon

BIG CATS ATTACK!

The domestic cat – cute, cuddly and king of YouTube – has 39 wild relatives whose awesome attributes are on a rather larger scale!

HIGHEST-LIVING PREDATOR ON LAND

The elusive snow leopard (left), native to Central Asia's rocky mountains, lives in some of the harshest conditions on Earth. It has been spotted at 5,800 m (19,000 ft) above sea level.

A puma, a fellow high-living feline, has also been recorded at similar altitudes in South America's Andes mountains.

11.7 m
The longest cat jump – a snow leopard's leap over a ditch – was recorded by Russian scientists (38 ft 4 in).

Uh-oh – could be the end of the lion for me! Think I'm gonna puma pants...

LARGEST WILD CAT

Found mainly in the boreal forest of eastern Russia, Siberian tigers can measure some 3.3 m (10 ft 9 in) from nose to tail tip and weigh around 300 kg (660 lb). One colossal specimen found in the Sikhote-Alin Gory mountains in 1950 tipped the scales at 384 kg (846 lb 9 oz) – that equates to roughly 100 pet cats!

KING OF THE CATS?

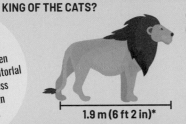 

*Length based on average for species, excluding the tail

A lion's mane provides built-in "chain mail" to protect its neck. Lions often fight as a group against territorial rivals, so they may be less ferocious than tigers in one-to-one combat.

1.9 m (6 ft 2 in)*   **2.9 m (9 ft 6 in)***

A big tiger will outweigh any lion. But whereas a lion "trains" for battle by play-fighting within a pride, the more solitary tiger can go its whole life without a serious big-cat encounter.

STRONGEST BIG-CAT BITE (RELATIVE TO BODY SIZE)

South America's largest cat, the jaguar, kills its prey with a bite to the neck or by piercing the skull with its formidable teeth. Wielding a force of up to 705 kg (1,554 lb), the fierce feline's jaws equip it to crack open turtle shells and even tackle caimans (right)!

LOWEST BIG-CAT ROAR

A lion roars in bouts lasting up to 90 sec. He can deliver 50 "calls" in that time, some with a frequency of 40 Hz – so deep that it's more of a vibration than a noise. Even from a mile away, the roars can be as loud as a car horn!

RAREST BIG CAT

Conservation efforts have more than doubled Amur leopard numbers in the last decade (see also p.145). But the total population of the **most northerly leopard subspecies** is still under 100. These critically endangered cats prowl mountainous forests along the China–Russia border.

see also p.145

To avoid having to share food, leopards sometimes... a) Haul it up a tree; b) Bury it; c) Hide it in a cave

SOUTH AMERICA

Some of this vast continent's desert habitats haven't seen rain for 400 years, but – just like its rainforests and tropical glaciers – they still teem with wildlife.

See **North America**, pp.28-29

(4) Most poisonous frog

Although it's smaller than a woman's thumb, a single golden poison-dart frog (see also p.132) contains enough toxin to kill 10 men! For centuries, the deadly liquid was used to tip hunters' blowgun darts, which is how this Colombian species earned its name.

(6) Heaviest snake

Green anacondas live in the swamps of tropical South America and Trinidad. One female, found in Brazil in 1960, was 8.4 m (27 ft 6 in) long and measured 1.1 m (3 ft 7 in) around – the same as a large man's chest. She weighed 500 lb (227 kg): heavier than three washing machines!

(9) Slowest mammal

The three-toed sloth (see p.42) moves so little that algae grows on its furry coat, giving it a greenish tint. It has a painfully slow walking speed, but in trees, where it spends most of its life, it can move twice as fast: up to 4.6 m (15 ft) per minute.

Most names for a mammal

In the English language alone, the puma has over 40 names including cougar, panther, mountain lion, painter, catamount (short for "cat-of-the-mountain") and deer tiger. Many sub-species also have their own names, such as Florida panther and Yuma cougar.

20

Largest toucan

The toco toucan can grow to a length of 65 cm (2 ft 1 in), a third of which is its enormous bill. This feature is made of keratin, which is what claws (and human fingernails) are formed of. The colourful beak includes air pockets too, so isn't as heavy as it looks.

29

Largest living bird of prey

The Andean condor has a wingspan of up to 3.2 m (10 ft 5 in), and can weigh as much as a four-year-old child. Being so heavy, it prefers to live in high, windy areas where it can glide on air currents. Condors are vultures, so feed mostly on carrion.

30

How many animals can you identify on this map? See pp.186–87 for answers.

139

TURTLE PARADISE

Raine Island on Australia's Great Barrier Reef has the **largest rookery of green turtles**. Up to 60,000 migrate thousands of kilometres to lay their eggs there in the breeding season, with more than 15,000 individuals nesting at any one time on the island's 1.8-km (1.1-mi) beach. Females lay 100–200 eggs at a time; two months later, the hatchlings emerge from the sand and crawl towards the ocean.

152

CONSERVATION CLUB

158

INTERVIEW
JANE GOODALL

In Jul 1960, at just 26 years old, primatologist Jane Goodall arrived in Tanzania to begin what is now the **longest-running wild primate study**. It's still going to this day.

Who or what led you to a career working with wildlife?

I was born loving animals. I read *Doctor Dolittle*, *The Jungle Book* and *Tarzan* when I was very young, and – aged 10 – decided that I would go to Africa, live with wild animals and write books about them.

Gombe in Tanzania, where you first started, is now a national park. What was it like when you first arrived?

I arrived with my mother, because at the time [1960] the authorities wouldn't let me work there on my own. Looking at the steep mountains and forested valleys, I wondered how I would ever find the chimps. But after we set up camp, I climbed a slope and sat looking out over Lake Tanganyika. Once I heard my first baboon bark, I was so excited!

Was there a turning point when you gained the chimps' trust and they accepted you?

For at least three months, the chimps ran off whenever I managed to find them. But one day I saw a group of about seven grooming and playing. I approached them carefully, but miscalculated distances and emerged from the vegetation much closer to them than I meant to. I thought they'd run, but to my amazement they looked up at me and just carried on. I was accepted. It was the proudest moment of my life.

How did you observe close-up without affecting the chimps' natural behaviour?

I never tried to get really close until they totally accepted me. Then it was often the chimps who approached me. Only when animals know you're there and aren't concerned can you be sure they're behaving normally.

Can you recall the very first time you witnessed chimps using tools?

I saw a chimp crouched over a termite mound. I watched him using grass stems to "fish" termites from their nest. I was amazed. Back then, it was thought that only humans made and used tools. As I watched, the chimp broke off a leafy twig and stripped off the leaves – modifying a natural object, the beginning of tool-making. After that, it was clear we had to redefine "man", redefine "tool" or accept chimps as human.

What aspects of chimp behaviour still need to be studied?

There's much to learn about different cultures in chimpanzee communities in different parts of Africa, and about the ways in which they can adapt to different circumstances. For example, chimps normally make nests in the evening and sleep in them all night. But chimps in Senegal, where it's very hot, may forage in the moonlight when it's cooler. Chimps in Uganda, driven to raid farmers' crops by their shrinking habitat, may also go out at night, when it's safer.

"Before I gained the chimps' trust and could get close to them, I sat on my perch high above the lake and made my observations remotely."

As a patron of Population Matters, tell us about how human population growth is affecting chimps.

Our population growth is a grave threat to future generations of chimps. People who need more land to grow food move deeper into the forests, clearing trees for farming. Often they take cattle and goats, which eat young seedlings. This causes the forest to gradually erode and become desert-like. People also bring new diseases into chimp territories – chimps are so like us biologically that they can catch our

ROOTS & SHOOTS (R&S)

"The message of R&S – a programme started with 12 high-school students in Tanzania in 1991 – is that everyone matters, has a role to play and can make a difference. We're putting that into practice here by planting a sapling at a local school."

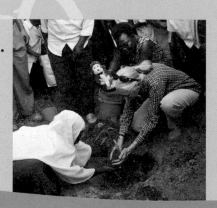

58
YEARS
Since Jane Goodall arrived at the reserve to study chimps, as of 2018

105
CHIMPS
Approximate chimp population at Gombe National Park

52 km²
Forested area that's protected: it's the smallest national park in Tanzania (20 sq mi)

200+
Species of bird that also call Gombe their home

1,500 m
Highest elevation above sea level in the reserve (4,920 ft)

"At first we used an ex-army tent that had no sewn-in groundsheet. Scorpions, snakes and all sorts of creatures could – and did! – come in."

fathers of the chimpanzees were. We can also use this technology to help understand diseases that affect chimpanzees, and hopefully to find ways to guard against them.

In conservation, we now use satellite imagery to understand how and where we're losing chimpanzee habitat. And we've trained forest rangers who use smartphones and tablets to monitor the forests on the ground. All this data helps the communities we work with decide how to manage their land.

Do you have advice for anyone considering a career in primatology?
First, follow the advice my mother gave me: "If you really want

something, work very hard, take advantage of opportunities and never give up!".

There are many educational programmes out there where you can study, but you can also just learn as much as you can, as I did, by reading books about animals. Even if you decide you don't want to pursue a career in animal behaviour, you can still find a way to make a difference, no matter what career path you take.

To find out about JGI's latest news and projects, visit **janegoodall.org** and **rootsandshoots.org**.

infectious diseases. There's often human-chimp conflict too, as chimps – having lost much of their forest – are forced to go raiding crops.

Why was the Jane Goodall Institute set up in 1977?
Some wonderful friends of mine established the Jane Goodall Institute [JGI] to ensure continued reliable funding for the research at Gombe. There are now dozens of branches around the world that raise money to help Gombe, as well as our other Africa programmes. Their work includes improving the lives of people living in and around chimp habitat, and caring for orphaned chimps.

How has the study of primates evolved?
We can do so much now by studying the animals' urine and faeces to understand family lineages, especially paternal relationships. Before, we never knew for sure who the

If you're Jane, does that make me Tarzan?!

THE WWF STORY

WWF (World Wide Fund for Nature) has been fighting to save habitats and wildlife on the brink since 1961. Here, we take a look at some of the charity's biggest milestones...

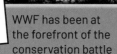

WWF has been at the forefront of the conservation battle for almost six decades. It has active projects – tackling everything from habitat loss to climate change – in 98 countries, plus 6,890 staff and some 5.4 million financial supporters, making it the **largest environmental conservation organization**.

With the giant panda symbolizing the charity, it's a testament to WWF's success that this species was downlisted from endangered to vulnerable in 2016. As WWF-UK's Chief Wildlife Advisor, Heather Sohl (see profile opposite), told us: "The number of giant pandas has increased by 16.8% in 10 years. This was due to great work across government, conservation groups, local people and scientists."

Saving the planet can be a very challenging job. But for WWF, with support from the public, scientists and other eco-minded organizations, it's just another day at the office.

WWF launches its first marine programme to protect turtle nesting sites (above), as well as to establish sanctuaries for whales and dolphins.

TIMELINE

1961
WWF is founded in response to threats of extinction being faced by iconic species worldwide.

Help to save the World's Wildlife

Your contribution will help to save the world's wildlife and wild places

Send it now to: World Wildlife Fund 2 Caxton Street London SW1

1972
WWF helps the Indian government to launch a six-year plan that leads to the creation of nine tiger reserves.

1975
WWF's first rainforest campaign results in dozens of national parks and reserves being established in Africa, Asia and Latin America.

1976

1990

WWF's global lobbying helps to secure an international ban on trade in ivory products.

What was the name of the panda that inspired WWF's logo? a) Wendy; b) Chi-Chi; c) Joy

WWF SUCCESS STORIES

WWF-led anti-poaching programmes have seen numbers of Amur leopard – the **rarest big cat** – more than double in recent years.

WWF played a key role in bringing Denmark, Norway, Canada, Russia and the USA together to commit to a 10-year action plan to manage and protect polar bears.

Thanks to a huge collaborative effort, poaching of greater one-horned rhinos has been all-but eradicated in Nepal and India.

WWF starts a successful campaign to protect UNESCO natural World Heritage Sites from harmful industrial activities.

WWF launches "Earth Hour", the annual lights-out, awareness-raising event that's now one of the largest environmental movements.

WWF's efforts contribute to the first increase in global wild tiger numbers in conservation history.

1993   2007   2013   2016

WWF helps to set up the Forest Stewardship Council (FSC) to promote responsible forestry around the world.

Inside the light and leafy Living Planet Centre, the home of WWF-UK.

GREEN HQ

In 2013, WWF-UK moved into brand-new premises in Woking, Surrey. Embodying the charity's values, the Living Planet Centre is – as far as possible – built of sustainably sourced and recyclable materials, making it one of the most eco-friendly offices in the UK. Features include recycled-carpet flooring, wind-assisted ventilation, solar panels and toilets flushed with waste water.

PROFILE: HEATHER SOHL,
Chief Wildlife Advisor, WWF-UK

What drew you to work for WWF?
I've been passionate about animals all my life and that's partly what drove me to work for an organization well known for wildlife conservation. I was even a WWF member when I was a child!

Is there an endangered species particularly close to your heart?
Tigers are a favourite. I'm about to move to a role where I'll focus on them. It's incredibly sad that this animal is so loved, yet its populations have declined by over 95% since the early 20th century.

What's it like to work in the field?
I've been lucky to meet some amazing people on my trips abroad. In Kenya's Maasai Mara, for example, I spent a night with the community rangers piloting thermal-imaging cameras. These help to see the heat signatures of poachers in the pitch black.

Are you striving towards a time when WWF is no longer needed?
We want a world where people and nature can thrive. Sadly, that isn't going to happen in the near future, but in the long-term, it's possible. It would put us out of a job, but we'd be okay with that!

Wild Things Editor, Adam Millward (right), with Heather Sohl (left) and WWF International Director of Brand Communications, Winnie De'ath (centre).

GUINNESS WORLD RECORDS

BIG PICTURE

Relative to adults, the **smallest baby for a mammal** – excluding marsupials and monotremes – is the newborn giant panda. They're not very giant at all, weighing in at 85–115 g (2.9–4 oz), which is less than a hamster. At birth, a panda cub is 1/900th the size of its mother!

40

Seconds that it takes a panda to peel and eat a bamboo shoot!

PANDA POWER

Widely recognized as the "poster bear" of WWF (see pp.144–45), China's giant panda is also a record holder on an epic scale.

The **hungriest bear**, it eats for up to 15 hr per day all year round – unlike other bears, who tend to slow down and eat less in the winter months. This endless chomping is necessary because the panda also has the **most restricted bear diet**: around 99% of its food is fairly innutritious bamboo! It's also the **most primitive living bear**, having diverged from all its bear relations between 18 and 25 million years ago.

IT'S ALL RELATIVE!

The **first panda known to science** was the smaller red panda from south-west China and the Himalayas. Named by French naturalist Georges-Frédéric Cuvier in 1825, tree-dwelling red pandas have raccoon-like ringed tails.

What colour is a panda's skin under its fur? a) Black and white; b) Blue and yellow; c) Black and pink

CONSERVATION CLUB

ATTENBOROUGH: A WILD LIFE

Since 1953, British naturalist Sir David Attenborough has brought the wild world into our living rooms. We take a look at some of the highlights of his TV career to date.

No other naturalist is as well-known as British national treasure Sir David Attenborough. Having enjoyed the **longest career as a TV presenter** – 64 years 122 days as of a *Blue Planet II* special episode broadcast on 1 Jan 2018 – his fame is hardly surprising!

Starting out in the early days of television in the 1950s, Sir David has truly stood the test of time. He's the only presenter to have won BAFTA awards for programmes in black and white, colour, HD *and* 3D.

His work has taken him hundreds of thousands of miles to some of the planet's remotest wildernesses to capture nature's great spectacles and amazing creatures on camera – all so that we can enjoy them from the comfort of our sofas.

Sir David feeds a mother orangutan in 1982, while her shy baby peeps out from under her arm!

Sir David is joined by two royal guests – Prince Charles and Princess Anne – as well as his pet cockatoo on *Zoo Quest* in 1958.

One of the highlights of *Blue Planet II* for Sir David was the episode "The Deep". This focused on rarely seen species such as the flapjack octopus (left), which can plunge to depths of 1,500 m (4,920 ft).

39 Countries visited while filming *Blue Planet II*, clocking up 6,000 hr of footage across 125 expeditions!

More than 10 million viewers tuned in to watch the first episode of *Blue Planet II*, which included a mother walrus and her baby in Svalbard, Norway.

Which animal does Sir David really not like? a) Rats; b) Spiders; c) Sharks

148

NAMED AFTER A LEGEND

The latest critter named in his honour is Attenborough's fan-throated lizard, described in 2018.

Attenborough's rubber frog – native to high peaks in Peru – was the first amphibian to be named after the record-breaking naturalist.

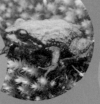

It's not all about animals... Sir David has also lent his name to flora, such as the Attenborough's pitcher plant of the Philippines.

PROFILE: SIR DAVID ATTENBOROUGH

Sir David poses with an atlas moth – a fellow record-breaker as the **largest moth** (see pp.84–85).

What drew you to a career working with wildlife?
I was inspired by American nature writer and artist Ernest Thompson Seton [a founding member of the Boy Scouts of America].

How did your TV career begin?
One of my first series was the BBC show *Zoo Quest* [see left] in 1954. I was filming an animal-collecting expedition that was sent out to Sierra Leone by London Zoo.

Which is the most challenging series you've worked on?
The most difficult show I have done was *Life on Earth*, which broadcast in 1979. It was a 13-part series that covered the whole animal and plant kingdom. It took three years to make and required travelling around the world not once, but twice!

If you could bring back one animal from extinction, what would it be?
Quetzalcoatlus, the **largest pterosaur** [see pp.102–03]. We make programmes about it, but we still don't know how it took off.

How can young people get more involved with conservation?
I'd recommend joining their local county wildlife trust.

ATTENBOROUGH TRIVIA

He'd like to spend a day as a sloth.
In a 2016 Twitter interview, Sir David confessed he was charmed by the slow creatures while filming *The Life of Mammals*. In the same Q&A, he revealed his favourite British animals are harvest mice and long-tailed tits.

Attenborough is *not* an "animal-lover".
Sir David has said on numerous occasions that he doesn't consider himself an "animal-lover" in the sense that implies sentiment. Rather, he finds animals "rivetingly interesting" and they give him a lot of "intellectual pleasure".

He keeps a yeti crab on his desk.
A paperweight containing one of the deep-sea critters (example right) is one of his most treasured possessions.

Attenborough's latest series, *Dynasty* – due to air in 2018 – focuses on individual animals at a key stage in their lives. Species to be covered include tigers, chimps and wild dogs.

In the final episode of *Blue Planet II*, Sir David got up close with leatherbacks, the **largest living turtles**.

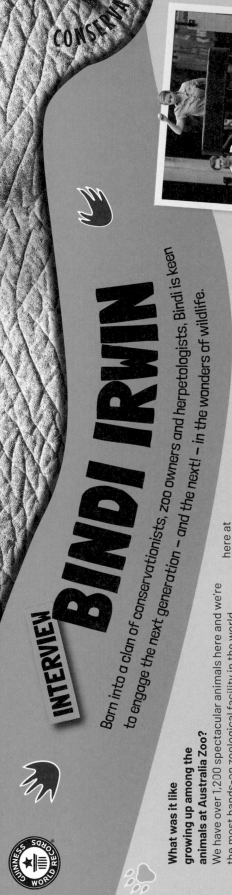

INTERVIEW

BINDI IRWIN

Born into a clan of conservationists, zoo owners and herpetologists, Bindi is keen to engage the next generation – and the next! – in the wonders of wildlife.

What was it like growing up among the animals at Australia Zoo?

We have over 1,200 spectacular animals here and we're the most hands-on zoological facility in the world, so every day brings new adventure! The best part of life at the zoo is sharing the wildlife with our visitors. You can meet almost all of our animals personally: cuddle koalas, kiss rhinos, scratch Komodo dragons, feed lemurs, hold birds and snakes…. I love watching our visitors connect with an animal. Once you do that, you want to learn more about it and protect it for the generations to come. That's what we're all about

here at
Australia Zoo. My dad
[conservationist, zookeeper and TV personality Steve Irwin] always said that people want to save the things they love. We follow this philosophy and try to break down barriers, dispelling the myths people may believe about many species.

How does it feel to be part of such a prestigious family of naturalists and conservationists?

Conservation work isn't just our job, it's who we are. I'm always learning from my family. We're a team no matter what, and together we hope to make a real difference on the planet for wildlife and wild places.

Your parents set up Wildlife Warriors Worldwide to involve people in supporting and conserving wildlife. What does being a Wildlife Warrior mean to you?

Being a Wildlife Warrior means speaking for those who can't speak for themselves. It's remembering that conservation is not just about cute and cuddly creatures, but also about wildlife such as crocodilians and sharks. Every species – from tiny jumping spiders to orangutans and turtles – has a special importance. All creatures need our respect, concern and protection.

What have Wildlife Warriors achieved so far?

We have conservation properties throughout Queensland that support at-risk species, such as

woma pythons, koalas and palm cockatoos. In western Queensland, one of our researchers has just completed his yakka skink project. These lizards are vulnerable, so we hope that studying their behaviour and habitat will help us to protect them better. Another Australian project is looking for a cure for devil facial tumour disease, which has caused a massive decline in the Tasmanian devil population.

Farther afield, we support cheetah and rhino conservation in Africa, tiger and elephant conservation in south-east Asia, and we're fighting for the protection of whales. I'm really

Australia Zoo's "Crococeum" was opened by Steve Irwin. Here, Bindi encourages a croc to "tail walk", a natural instinct for wild crocodiles.

Pictured here as a baby with her dad Steve, Bindi was introduced to formidable creatures such as the Burmese python from an early age.

So you're sure he's already had his lunch? And what about the snake?

"Always stand up for what you believe in!"

"Volunteer at conservation organizations to get more involved."

"Read all you can! This is the advice I was given and it applies to everything in life. There's no limit to the knowledge you can gain from avidly reading."

pleased with breakthroughs we've made against the illegal hunting and trade of Sumatran tigers. We're proud to have raised millions of dollars, all of which goes directly back into conservation work.

Where do you see Wildlife Warriors in 50 years' time?

Our mission is to make the world a better place for future generations – to ensure that we always have clean air, fresh drinking water and an abundance of wildlife. Every time we lose an animal species, it's like losing a brick from a house: if we keep that up, eventually the house will fall down. In 50 years, the Wildlife Warriors will still be working to protect wild species and places, but I hope that by then we'll have curbed the extinction rate.

AUSTRALIA ZOO WILDLIFE HOSPITAL

Working with research teams across Australia, Wildlife Warriors are helping to save one of the country's national icons. The hospital's first priority is to provide life-saving treatment to sick and injured wild koalas. Below, a six-month-old koala, too young to be separated from his injured mother, clings to her during a check-up. With the help of her super-supportive joey, she made a full recovery. To find out more about Wildlife Warriors, check out **wildlifewarriors.org.au.**

Who inspires you in the field of wildlife conservation?

Dad was truly the ultimate Wildlife Warrior. He inspired millions of people around the world to love wildlife and want to make a difference. He will always be my greatest inspiration and his legacy will live on forever.

Do you miss Australian animals when you're away from home?

When we're travelling abroad, I miss echidnas the most. They're such unusual animals, one of only two known egg-laying mammals [monotremes], the other being the platypus. It's fun to feed them at the zoo: their long tongues tickle when they lick food off your hands! But I love spending time with North American species, too. Opossums are one of the most misunderstood animals in the USA – they're actually super-sweet. I knew one who loved cuddles and kisses.

Where in the world is your favourite place to see wildlife?

I personally love Tasmania for spotting the best wildlife. Cradle Mountain National Park is a hotspot for all the best Aussie native animals. You can watch platypus playing in the creeks, meet wombats and echidnas wandering down your path, see Tasmanian devils growling and pademelons hopping everywhere. It's spectacular and truly the land that time forgot.

AUSTRALIA ZOO WILDLIFE WARRIORS

CONSERVATION CLUB

ALL ABOUT ORANGUTANS

These intelligent great apes, found only in the rainforests of Borneo and Sumatra, spend almost their entire lives hanging about in trees.

BORNEAN ORANGUTAN

SCIENTIFIC NAME: *Pongo pygmaeus*

TYPE: Mammal

HEIGHT (MALE): 1.3–1.5 m (4 ft 3 in–4 ft 11 in)

WEIGHT (MALE): 75–83 kg (165–183 lb)

DIET: Omnivore, e.g., fruit, seeds, insects, eggs

LIFESPAN: 35–45 years

RANGE: Borneo

97% DNA that orangutans share with humans, surpassed only by bonobos (over 98%) and chimpanzees (99%).

"Orang" and "utan" are the Malay words for "person" and "forest", so an orangutan is literally a "person of the forest". Its expressive face and resourcefulness (using a chewed leaf as a sponge, for example, or a stick as a honey-dip) makes the human link pretty clear. But these great apes – the **largest tree-dwelling mammals** – have little need to venture to the ground, where their hand-like feet and long arms make walking awkward. The two known orangutan species – Bornean and Sumatran – were joined by a third in 2017. The Tapanuli orangutan (see pp.90–91) lives in northern Sumatra.

GREAT GRIP

Like us, orangutans have four fingers and an opposable thumb on each hand.
Unlike us, they also have opposable big toes!

CHEEKY CHOPS

Some males grow thick pads of flesh, known as "flanges", that frame their faces. Females seem to find males who have them more attractive than those who don't.

A LONG STRETCH

An orangutan's powerful arms are one-and-a-half times longer than its legs. This makes it well adapted to swinging in the trees.

GUINNESS WORLD REC

ANTISOCIAL CLIMBERS

Adult males almost always live alone, while adult females travel with their most recent baby and perhaps one other youngster.

King Louie in Disney's 2016 film *The Jungle Book* is based on the extinct primate *Gigantopithecus*, which may have stood over 3 m (9 ft 10 in) tall.

Orangutans use an assortment of vocalizations. Some – such as their laughter when they're playing or being tickled – are similar to those of humans.

RED ALERT

Orangutans' greyish-black skin is mostly covered with wispy hair. Sumatran apes often have lighter, redder coats compared with their Bornean cousins.

PROFILE: LONGEST–RUNNING ORANGUTAN REHAB CENTRE

Since the Sepilok Orangutan Rehabilitation Centre opened in Borneo in 1964, it has released more than 300 rescued orphans back into the wild, according to Sepilok's Wildlife Officer, Sylvia Alsisto. Today, there are around 100 orangutans in the rainforest reserve. Sepilok uses a "buddy system" to replace a mother's teaching: an infant is paired with an older ape, helping the younger one to develop the skills it needs.

LIVING IT LARGE

There's a huge difference in size between male and female orangutans: an adult male may be three times as heavy as his female counterpart.

BENDY BODIES

Super-mobile hip and shoulder joints make orangutans more flexible than humans and other apes.

WHERE IN THE WORLD?

SUMATRA AND BORNEO, INDONESIA

The south-east Asian islands of Borneo and Sumatra are home to some of the most biologically diverse rainforests on Earth. The world's third and sixth largest islands respectively, they host thousands of species found nowhere else, including the last remaining pygmy elephants, Sumatran tigers, Sumatran rhinos – and, of course, orangutans.

INTERVIEW
NISHA OWEN

EDGE of Existence is a conservation programme with a difference. Here, its lead scientist sets out how the new initiative is shaking up old ideas about saving animals.

How did the EDGE of Existence programme start?

The Zoological Society of London [ZSL] is an international conservation and charity founded – amazingly – as long ago as 1826. Its mission was (and

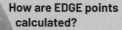
Nisha hangs out with the **smallest sloth** on the island of Escudo de Veraguas, Panama.

still is) to promote and achieve the conservation of animals and their habitats all over the world.

In 2007, scientists from ZSL's Institute of Zoology invented a new way of analysing which endangered species most need help. It's a points-based system called the EDGE metric. It's based on the unique evolutionary history of a species, as well as its risk of extinction. The evolutionary history is really important because some species – the ones EDGE identifies – represent entire branches of the tree of life. If those species are on the verge of extinction, we risk a hugely significant loss. Extinction of any species is desperately sad, of course, but losing these priority species is unthinkable.

How are EDGE points calculated?

We draw up an evolutionary tree for the species, which sets out how many millions of years' history that species represents. Then we look at the Red List maintained by the International Union for Conservation of Nature [IUCN], which assesses how endangered a species is. Categories range from "Least Concern" to "Critically Endangered". We combine the results to establish EDGE scores.

Bactrian camels are one of the EDGE species at London Zoo, UK. In their native Gobi desert, they can go for days without food or drink.

We've now identified the "top 100" species that need priority attention.

What's the most endangered species on EDGE's current lists?

Unfortunately, there are many mammals, birds, amphibians, reptiles and corals on the lists. We highlight those that are receiving the least conservation attention but are most in need – such as the vaquita. These little porpoises, the **rarest cetaceans**, are found only in the Gulf of California off north-eastern Mexico, and there may be fewer than 30 individuals left.

Another one on the list is the Chinese giant salamander, which – at up to 1.8 m [5 ft 10 in] – is the **largest amphibian** [see pp.66–67]. This amazing creature can grow as large as an adult human, though its tadpoles are just 2.5 cm [1 in] long. The species used to be widespread across China, but recent surveys have found only a handful of them left in the wild.

"The hooded grebe of Patagonia is threatened by climate change as well as invasive predators such as the American mink."

"India's purple pig-nosed frog is my favourite amphibian. Discovered only in 2003, it spends most of its life underground."

"There are fewer than 100 pygmy sloths in the wild, on just one island near Panama. I've been lucky enough to meet some of them in the (hairy) flesh [see opposite]."

What are the highlights of EDGE's first decade (2007–17)?

Much of our success is down to the work of our Fellows – conservationists we've helped to train. Many of them work in countries that are rich in biodiversity but have limited resources. So far we've trained 79 Fellows in 40 countries, and their successes have been many and varied. They've established protected areas, implemented new laws and targeted key threats. Some have uncovered new populations of species – such as the Ghanaian Togo slippery frog – and one team discovered a Kenyan elephant shrew that might even be new to science!

One of our latest projects is the mapping of "EDGE Zones", which will help to identify priority landscapes for conservation.

How do you track down a species that might be extinct?

It's certainly not easy – I can report only mixed success!

A month-long expedition looking for long-beaked echidna in the Cyclops Mountains of Papua New Guinea, for example, involved travelling to parts of the jungle-covered mountain range that had remained unexplored for more than 45 years. We uncovered burrows and tracks made by this egg-laying mammal, and heard reports of sightings by local people... but so far we haven't found a live specimen.

On the other hand, we have spotted the Cebu flowerpecker bird in the Philippines, which was feared to be extinct.

74
Number of EDGE species that Fellows have helped to conserve since the programme began in 2007.

Does the EDGE programme involve reintroducing animals?

Not yet – mostly because many of the species we highlight are so little known. The first step is often to establish their status – their range, population size and key threats – and then we're in a better position to work out how we can help them.

Do you think that conservationists can sometimes get blinkered by animal "poster stars"?

Well, perhaps "distracted" would be a better word than "blinkered" – some creatures, after all, do capture the imagination more easily than others! Mainstream conservation does tend to focus largely on charismatic or culturally important animals, though, which are mostly large mammals.

We provide a complementary approach, making sure that we direct conservation efforts beyond the usual suspects. That said, some of the most high-profile mammals, such as giant pandas and elephants, are also EDGE species.

EDGE

AYE-AYES ON THE PRIZE

ZSL zoos are home to a number of EDGE species, including pygmy hippos, northern bald ibises and aye-ayes (above), the **largest nocturnal primates**. London Zoo's aye-ayes are kept in a special enclosure that mimics night-time conditions during the day, so that they're more active. The pair recently had a baby, though spotting him in the dark is a real challenge!

Can members of the public contribute to the EDGE programme?

Definitely! We encourage everyone to raise awareness and share knowledge of EDGE species. You can also donate to our work at **www.edgeofexistence.org**.

What should tomorrow's conservationists be studying?

Conservationists come from a variety of backgrounds. The traditional science subjects are a brilliant start, but you could also become a conservationist by studying economics or even law, because conservation is about people too. And if your strengths are in the arts – well, where would we be without talented creative people to get the message across?

ZSL is helping to save rare reptiles such as the Annam leaf turtle, found only in Vietnam, by working with the Asian Turtle Program.

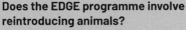

URBAN WILDLIFE

As natural environments are squeezed by expanding cities, some species are fighting back, moving in and making the most of human habitats.

When "townies" cultivate their patches of green to provide food, water and places to nest, urban landscapes can become wildlife oases. Parks, gardens and allotments – as well as unkempt corners and abandoned woodpiles [see "The Bug Hotel", pp.86–87] – play host to city critters that keep their human neighbours connected to nature.

21

Number of days it takes a newborn falcon to reach 10 times its birth weight.

Peregrine falcons achieve the **fastest dive by a bird**, reaching some 300 km/h (186 mph). They nest high on cliff ledges – or in cities, on skyscrapers and cathedral spires from where they swoop on passing pigeons (see below).

Pigeons' wild ancestors are rock doves, natives of sea cliffs and mountains. So, unlike many birds, they're perfectly adapted to an urban terrain.

The **largest fox**, the red fox, is an adaptable creature that flourishes in built-up areas where gardens provide hiding places as well as food. Urban foxes may once have been rural dwellers that strayed into cities, but since they can travel long distances, they're now probably "commuters" – spreading from town to town.

RED FOX

SCIENTIFIC NAME: *Vulpes vulpes*

TYPE: Mammal

LENGTH: 45–90 cm (1 ft 5 in–2 ft 11 in)

WEIGHT: Up to 14 kg (30 lb 13 oz)

DIET: Omnivore, e.g., insects, garbage, rats, birds

LIFESPAN: 2–5 years

RANGE: Northern hemisphere

DAVID'S TOP CITY CRITTERS

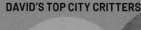

"The opossum, the **most northerly marsupial** and North America's only marsupial, is always welcome since it feeds on rodents and venomous snakes."

"I'm particularly partial to gray tree frogs because I love amphibians – and these guys have really cool camouflage patterns."

BUGS TO LIFE!
GO TO PP. 88-89

"The gorgeous monarch – which performs the **longest butterfly migration** [see p.89] – has declined hugely, mostly because of our overuse of insecticides."

GUINNESS WORLD RECORDS

We just love dropping in for a capuchino!

The pink-stone Temple of Galtaji in Jaipur, India, is dedicated to the Hindu monkey god, Hanuman. Named after the god and considered sacred by some, Hanuman langurs belong to the **largest monkey family**, Cercopithecidae.

Raccoons have taken so well to city life that they're now more common in North American cities than in the countryside

With powerful jaws and advanced senses, spotted hyenas are the **most efficient scavengers**. In the Ethiopian city of Harar, these wild visitors are revered for clearing up unwanted scraps – even bones!

PROFILE: DAVID MIZEJEWSKI, nature presenter & author

What inspired you to be a naturalist?
I was born that way! From as early as I can remember, I was always drawn to animals and the natural world. By the time I was in college, I knew that working in wildlife conservation was my life's calling.

What's your role with the National Wildlife Federation (NWF)?
I help interpret the workings of the natural world and wildlife in a way that inspires people to get involved in conservation. I also manage several of NWF's social media channels and work with staff across the organization to ensure scientific accuracy.

Is there as much urban wildlife today as there was in the past?
Yes and no. Wildlife populations are declining, but some species are adapting to human urbanization. These are the animals – such as raccoons, opossums, northern cardinals, coyote and even black bear and white-tailed deer – that can take advantage of a wide range of habitat types and food resources.

Which species are the most surprising to find in cities?
Probably coyotes. With wolves out of the picture, coyotes – smaller, much more adaptable canids – have dramatically expanded their range.

How does urban wildlife differ across cities/regions in the USA?
The range of wildlife depends on climate, plant cover, food sources – and the level of human persecution – just as it does in wild areas. In the Pacific Northwest, you might encounter a beaver; in Texas, you can see flights of Mexican free-tailed bats; in New England, moose may wander into town; while in Florida people sometimes find an alligator in their backyard!

What can people do to make their backyards more wildlife-friendly?
Each of us can create a space that supports birds, bees, butterflies and other "backyard wildlife", be it on a balcony or among rural acreage. It's as simple as planting native plants and providing sources of food, water, cover and places to raise young. Keep it as natural as possible and you'll be doing your bit for both local species and the migrators that pass through our cities and towns.

NATIONAL WILDLIFE FEDERATION · SINCE 1936 ·

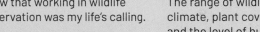

To help them navigate, foxes have whiskers on their faces and on their... a) Ankles; b) Backs; c) Tongues

CONSERVATION CLUB

ANIMAL LOLS

The Comedy Wildlife Photography Awards, dedicated to promoting "conservation through competition", prove that conservation *can* be a laughing matter!

PROFILE: TIBOR KÉRCZ,
Winner of The Comedy Wildlife
Photography Awards, 2017

Is photography work or a hobby?
Nature and wildlife photography are big passions of mine – I spend all my free time outdoors. I'm actually a chemical engineer by profession.

Which was your favourite 2017 entry (excluding your own)?
The penguins marching to the church [inset below]. I hope they went to pray for a colder climate!

How did you capture the winning photos?
The images were taken close to a farm in southern Hungary. The nestlings were practising take-off techniques. I was already in my hide-tent when one of them started to lose its balance – you can see what happened next!

Your prize is a safari in Kenya. What do you hope to see?
I'm most looking forward to seeing – and photographing – the wildebeest migration, especially through the Mara River.

Overall Winner 2017
"Help" (sequence of four)
by Tibor Kércz

Highly Commended
"All Dressed and Ready for Church" by Carl Henry

OMG!
There are as many as 15 million little owls on Earth. It's the **most abundant** owl.

The Comedy Wildlife PHOTOGRAPHY AWARDS

Set up in 2014, The Comedy Wildlife Photography Awards are a fun way of drawing attention to animals in need. In 2017, there were entries from 86 countries.

The top prize in 2015 went to "Rush Hour" by Julian Rad.

Angela Bohlke's foxy fail, "A Tough Day at the Office", was the overall winner of 2016's contest.

Highly Commended
"Eh What's Up Doc?"
by Olivier Colle

Ha ha, I win again at hide and squeak!

Highly Commended
"Mudskippers Got Talent"
by Daniel Trim

Winner,
"On the Land" category
"The Laughing Dormouse"
by Andrea Zampatti

Highly Commended
"Monkey Escape"
by Katy Laveck-Foster

Mudskipper fish, which can live outside water, have an odd walking style that is known as... a) Crutching; b) Bumshuffling; c) Slytherin

159

INTERVIEW
ROBERT IRWIN

The youngest of the Irwin wildlife dynasty, 14-year-old Robert reveals how he uses photography to see animals in a new light and to inspire others into conservation.

Do you have a favourite animal or species at Australia Zoo?

My favourite would definitely be crocodiles. Crocs have always fascinated me – it's incredible that they've existed on the planet for over 200 million years, having survived through extinctions that wiped out most other life. They're very intelligent creatures and truly are modern-day dinosaurs. It's so much fun working with them at the zoo because you can see each croc's individual personality.

Who first inspired you to pick up a camera?

I've been passionate about photography for quite a while now. It started from taking photos on a little digital point-and-shoot camera when I was about six years old. One of my biggest inspirations is my dad: he loved photography and took his camera gear on all of his travels. My goal in life is to continue his legacy and my family's amazing conservation work through my wildlife photography.

Do you think wildlife photography and conservation go hand in hand?

Oh, yes – they definitely do. Photography is a great way of inspiring others about issues facing our planet, because each image tells a story about its subject. Photography is also a way to showcase magnificent creatures and places that many people won't have the opportunity to see for themselves, and – I hope – inspire them to want to conserve these irreplaceable wonders.

What are the main challenges of wildlife photography?

You never quite know what's going to happen when you're photographing wild animals! It's huge fun, but certainly requires patience.

I've been very lucky and visited extraordinary places around the world, photographing in all kinds of weather conditions to capture images of animals in their natural home. Sometimes you have to wait for days to get one good photo, and other times something incredible happens when you least expect it. It's a challenge, but that makes it really rewarding when you get a great shot.

Which of your photos are you most proud of and why?

It's tough to pick just one, because so many of them have a big story behind them. But perhaps the photo I'm

Robert puts his photography skills to good use, snapping crocs at Steve Irwin Wildlife Reserve in Queensland as part of an annual survey.

most proud of is one I took a couple of years ago of the last male northern white rhino [see bottom left].

Wildlife Warriors [read more on pp.150–51] supports conservation projects all over the world including the protection of wild rhinos at the Ol Pejeta Conservancy in Kenya. We went there to take a look at the great work they're doing, and I had the honour of meeting Sudan, who was then one of only three northern white rhinos left. He was kept under armed protection in a semi-wild situation.

ROBERT'S TOP SNAPS

At the Ol Pejeta wildlife conservancy in central Kenya, Robert photographed Sudan (left), the last male northern white rhino. Sudan was something of a celebrity in his lifetime, attracting visitors from all over the world.

Robert snorkelled alongside humpback whales (right) off Lady Elliot Island, at the tip of Australia's Great Barrier Reef.

ROBERT'S WILDLIFE PHOTOGRAPHY TIPS

"No matter where you live or what gear you have, you can capture images of animals in their environment and experiment with new techniques."

"Connect with your subject. If you learn about the behaviour of the animals you photograph and try to understand them, you'll get even better photos."

"Don't forget to enjoy the experience! After you get a good shot of an animal, put the camera down for a while and just enjoy watching them."

In photography, koalafications are irrelephant – you just need a worthwhale sense of porpoise!

Toddler Robert with his mum Terri, dad Steve and sister Bindi (see pp.150–51). Robert's grandparents opened the family zoo in 1970.

in their habitat, facing extreme temperatures, harsh terrain, severe weather events, competition from other animals and the ever-present threat of humans.

How does it feel to see your work hanging in galleries?
It's such an honour. Not only is it important to record wildlife, but it's also great to be able to share it with people, helping – I hope – to inspire a larger audience.

Tell us about your most memorable photography expedition so far.
I've been lucky enough to photograph all over the world, but one of the most memorable expeditions was to Lady Elliot Island on the southern end of the Great Barrier Reef in Queensland, Australia. While I was snorkelling in the deep water, two humpback whales [see opposite, bottom right] emerged from the gloomy depths and swam right up to me. It took my breath away to be so close to them. They swam around for about half an hour before disappearing back into the deep water. It was an experience that I'll never forget.

It was very moving to spend time with him and photograph him. Sadly, Sudan died, aged 45, in 2018. Northern white rhinos have been wiped out in the wild because of poaching. I hope that the photo gives an idea of how incredible he was and why it's vital to conserve other rhino species.

Wildlife Warriors was set up to get people involved in conservation. Why should people sign up?
We need Wildlife Warriors in order to conserve our natural world, and we need to inspire young people – the next generation – in particular. Anyone can make a difference, but if we all play our part then we can have a world with abundant wildlife and wild places.

Does photographing animals offer us a unique insight into their lives?
Definitely. It's always amazing to observe how animals adapt and survive

10
Age at which Robert first fed a saltwater croc at Australia Zoo's "Crocoseum".

Which species are still on your "must-photograph" list?
There are so many! Komodo dragons are certainly pretty high on the list. My dad worked with them in the wild on Komodo Island, and I've always dreamed of photographing them there in their natural habitat.

Robert and his sister appeared in which 2010 movie? a) *Free Willy: Escape from Pirate's Cove*; b) *Toy Story 3*; c) *Inception*

ANTARCTICA

This frozen land has barely any vegetation and the **coldest temperatures on Earth** (−89.2°C; −128.6°F). It's hard to imagine anything surviving here, but a few hardy animals have found a way...

Fastest swimming bird
No other bird is faster in water than the gentoo penguin, clocked swimming at short bursts of 36 km/h (22 mph). They leap out of the water to catch their breath and also to avoid predators – a manoeuvre known as "porpoising".

Largest carnivore
Reaching the length of a car and the weight of two hippos, male southern elephant seals (bulls) even dwarf polar bears! The females (cows), by contrast, can be as much as eight times lighter. They live mainly on the shores of sub-Antarctic islands.

Largest land animal in Antarctica
Several seal and penguin species pass many months on the icy fringes of the Antarctic, but a lot of their time is spent in the water. On the continent itself, the biggest permanent resident (excluding human scientists) is the tiny 1.2-cm (0.4-in) Antarctic midge!

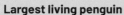

Largest living penguin
Emperor penguins stand 1.3 m (4 ft 3 in) tall, about the same height as an eight-year-old child. They huddle in colonies that can be 20,000 strong. A 2018 study reported on a tagged emperor penguin diving in the Ross Sea for 32.2 min – the **longest underwater dive by a bird**.

12

11

15

Fastest marine mammal
Orcas, aka killer whales, have been recorded reaching speeds of 55.5 km/h (34.5 mph), which is faster than a galloping horse. These pack hunters, the **largest dolphin species**, have been known to exhaust their prey by chasing it for hours.

21

12

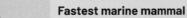

16

19

21

20

17

13

22

14

18

Heaviest colossal squid
Cold Antarctic waters are far richer in oxygen than those in warmer climes. This could be one of the major reasons why polar sealife grows extra-large. A colossal squid (right) found in the Ross Sea by fishermen in 2007 tipped the scales at 495 kg (1,091 lb).

22

How many animals can you identify on this map? See pp.186–87 for answers.

THE UBER-ZOO

Based on the number of species that live there, Zoo Berlin in Germany is the world's **largest zoo**. The 35-ha (86-acre) site, which includes an aquarium, an aviary and the modern, glass-domed Hippo House (main picture and inset), looks after more than 19,000 animals from 1,354 different species. These include lions, gorillas, penguins and the country's only giant pandas.

180

ZOOTOPIA

178

ZOO BABIES

Animal parks and zoos around the world are reporting successes in breeding rare and endangered species. All these new arrivals made their parents proud in 2017–18.

1

3

2

4

5

When a litter of African painted pups is born, the whole pack pitches in to help raise them.

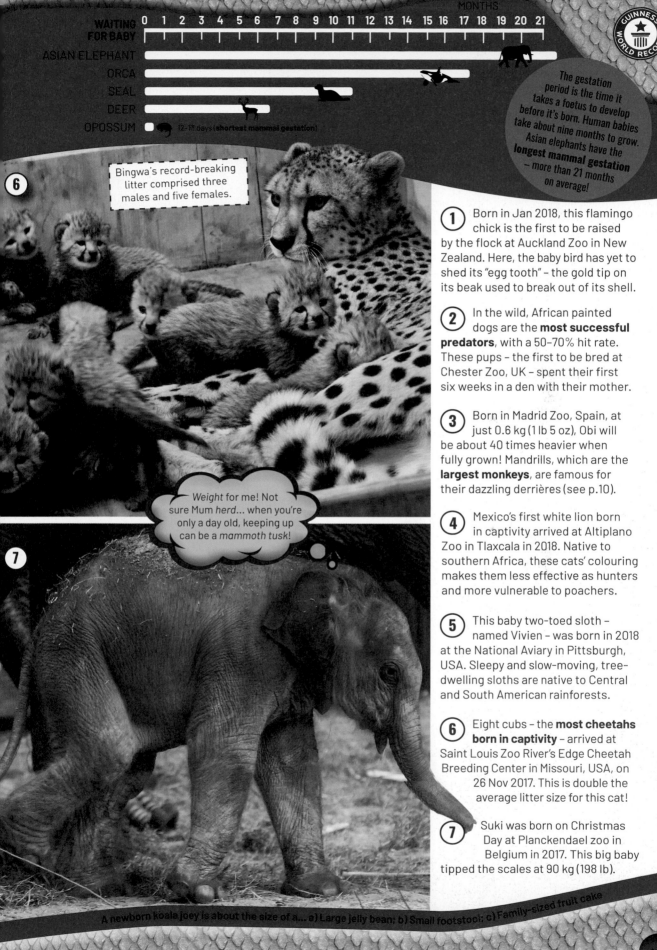

WAITING FOR BABY

	0	1	2	3	4	5	6	7	8	9	10	11	12	13	14	15	16	17	18	19	20	21

ASIAN ELEPHANT

ORCA

SEAL

DEER

OPOSSUM — 12–13 days (shortest mammal gestation)

The gestation period is the time it takes a foetus to develop before it's born. Human babies take about nine months to grow. Asian elephants have the **longest mammal gestation** – more than 21 months on average!

6

Bingwa's record-breaking litter comprised three males and five females.

Weight for me! Not sure Mum herd... when you're only a day old, keeping up can be a mammoth tusk!

7

1 Born in Jan 2018, this flamingo chick is the first to be raised by the flock at Auckland Zoo in New Zealand. Here, the baby bird has yet to shed its "egg tooth" – the gold tip on its beak used to break out of its shell.

2 In the wild, African painted dogs are the **most successful predators**, with a 50–70% hit rate. These pups – the first to be bred at Chester Zoo, UK – spent their first six weeks in a den with their mother.

3 Born in Madrid Zoo, Spain, at just 0.6 kg (1 lb 5 oz), Obi will be about 40 times heavier when fully grown! Mandrills, which are the **largest monkeys**, are famous for their dazzling derrières (see p.10).

4 Mexico's first white lion born in captivity arrived at Altiplano Zoo in Tlaxcala in 2018. Native to southern Africa, these cats' colouring makes them less effective as hunters and more vulnerable to poachers.

5 This baby two-toed sloth – named Vivien – was born in 2018 at the National Aviary in Pittsburgh, USA. Sleepy and slow-moving, tree-dwelling sloths are native to Central and South American rainforests.

6 Eight cubs – the **most cheetahs born in captivity** – arrived at Saint Louis Zoo River's Edge Cheetah Breeding Center in Missouri, USA, on 26 Nov 2017. This is double the average litter size for this cat!

7 Suki was born on Christmas Day at Planckendael zoo in Belgium in 2017. This big baby tipped the scales at 90 kg (198 lb).

A newborn koala joey is about the size of a... a) Large jelly bean; b) Small footstool; c) Family-sized fruit cake

SENIOR CITIZENS

With age comes not just respect, but also records! Though these oldies have far exceeded their species' average lifespan, they show little sign of slowing down...

SEA OTTER

Charlie, the **oldest living sea otter**, celebrated his 21st birthday in 2018 with a party and a special shrimp and clam cake – *yum!* He was found stranded as a cub in 1997 and has lived at the Aquarium of the Pacific in California, USA, since. Male sea otters in the wild usually live for 10–15 years.

ICELANDIC SEA EAGLE

When an injured bird was brought into the Icelandic Natural History Museum in Reykjavík in 2018, staff discovered that it had been tagged in Breiðafjörður bay, Iceland, in 1993. That meant it was at least 25 years old – four years older than the species' average lifespan – making it the **oldest Icelandic sea eagle** on record.

Gorgeous, aren't I? Still a natural redhead after all these years...

SUMATRAN ORANGUTAN

Puan has lived at Perth Zoo in Australia since 1968, when she was about 12. The **oldest living Sumatran orangutan**, she celebrated her 62nd birthday in 2018 – or her keepers did, anyway... Puan herself reportedly spent her big day avoiding the kerfuffle by hiding under a sack!

Puan has had 11 children and is a great-grandmother, having exceeded the usual orangutan life expectancy of 50 years.

OLDEST EVER...

	YEARS
	0 10 20 30 40 50 60 70 80 90 100
ELEPHANT	
MANATEE	
BROWN BEAR	
GIANT PANDA	
WOMBAT	

Each animal on the chart is the **oldest ever** of its species in captivity. The super-seniors are: Asian elephant Lin Wang (86 years); manatee Snooty (69 years 2 days); Andreas the brown bear (50 years); panda Jia Jia (38 years); and wombat Patrick (31 years 107 days).

Jonathan – here a "youngster" at around 54 years of age – chills with chums back in 1886, when Queen Victoria was still on the throne!

Age has tortoise to shellebrate every century like it's our last!

SEYCHELLES GIANT TORTOISE

Jonathan is the **oldest living land animal**. It's thought that he was born in 1832, which would make him 186 years old in 2018!

Jonathan lives on the island of St Helena in the South Atlantic, in a paddock at the bottom of the Governor's garden. He lives with three other tortoises, and his healthy diet includes carrots, cucumber and bananas. In 2016, he enjoyed his first-ever bath – or top-to-tail shell-scrub – in preparation for a royal visit.

Just off to an old friend's for a quick bite!

AMERICAN ALLIGATOR

Muja, the **oldest alligator in captivity**, lives at Belgrade Zoo in Serbia. He arrived fully grown in Sep 1937, so by 2018 he was at least 80 years old. The zoo was almost destroyed during World War II bombings: Muja is the only survivor from that time.

POLAR BEAR: IN FOND MEMORY...

In early 2018, Coldilocks of Philadelphia Zoo in Pennsylvania, USA, was the **oldest living polar bear in captivity**. On her 37th birthday, she partied and feasted on a special peanut butter and fish birthday-bear cake.

Sadly, Coldilocks died in Feb 2018, so her record no longer stands. But she is fondly remembered, and far surpassed a polar bear's average 23-year lifespan.

Which body part is often used to estimate the age of an elephant? a) its tail; b) its feet; c) its teeth

WEIGH-IN AT THE ZOO

Pygmy goats, Asiatic lions and Humboldt penguins were just some of the animals to be measured up when ZSL London Zoo held its annual stats-fest in 2017.

ZSL London Zoo is home to some 20,000 residents. Keeping tabs on each animal's vital statistics is crucial to monitor its health and diet. Weight is especially important: with luck, an expanding waistline might indicate a new baby on the way!

Once a year, figures are updated at a grand weigh-in, and then shared with zoos and conservationists across the world. Keepers use ingenious tactics – bribery with treats or distraction with toys – to persuade their charges to cooperate. But sometimes the animals have other ideas...

kg
15.8

Pygmy goats proved to be just as stubborn as their bigger cousins – but Ellie eventually stepped up to the plate for a snack!

kg
1.23

A coloured ball on a stick keeps this squirrel monkey on the scales for just long enough to log its weight...

kg
4.25

A Humboldt penguin obligingly steps on the weighing machine in the breakfast queue.

The heaviest creature at the 2017 weigh-in was Ellish the giraffe. She registered 850 kg (1,873 lb 14 oz) and stands 4.5 m (15 ft) tall.

ZSL London Zoo's lightest creature is a leafcutter ant, which tips the teeny scales at just 3–5 mg (0.0001– 0.0002 oz).

ZSL London Zoo contained the **first children's zoo**. It was opened in 1938 by six-year-old Teddy Kennedy from the USA, who later became Senator Edward Kennedy of Massachusetts.

118 kg

A hanging sack full of meat tempts an Asiatic lioness to stand tall in order to record her length.

Fea's flying tree frogs weigh about the same as a pack of playing cards. Using the webbing on their feet to sustain their "flight", some flying frog species can glide 15 m (50 ft), making them the **farthest gliding amphibians**.

092 g

1.41 kg

The male spiny hill turtle weighed about 30 g (1 oz) more than the female. Above is their average weight.

Western lowland gorillas, native to central Africa, are among today's **largest primates** – only surpassed by their eastern lowland cousins. ZSL London Zoo's silverback, Kumbuka, stands as tall as a man but weighs more than twice as much. Scientists estimate that the wild population of these gorillas has declined by more than 60% since the 1990s.

185 kg

OMG! An adult gorilla's daily food weighs about the same as a six-year-old child!

4

3

2

Which gorilla feature is sometimes used to identify individuals? a) Nose; b) Bottom; c) Ears

SUPER ZOOS

Zoos and wildlife parks around the world are finding increasingly creative ways to promote conservation while making animals feel right at home!

LARGEST WALK-THROUGH ZOO

North Carolina Zoo in the Uwharrie Mountains, USA, is home to more than 1,600 animals from more than 250 different species. Set across 2,200 acres (890 ha), with around 5 mi (8 km) of trails, this is the biggest zoo that visitors can explore by foot. Some 500 acres (202 ha) are given to "natural habitat" enclosures that are designed to recreate wild terrain, including forest, ponds and grassland.

Grizzly bears enjoy a dip in their very own pool.

Scarlet ibis generally wait for summer before taking their turn in the pool.

LARGEST OPEN-RANGE ZOO

Monarto Zoological Park – located 70 km (43 mi) from South Australia's capital, Adelaide – spans more than 3,700 acres (1,500 ha). The safari park includes several major habitat zones, including African plains, North African arid terrain, Asian grasslands and Asian steppes. It's also involved in conservation projects for endangered native Australian species, such as the fat-tailed dunnart (inset), a tiny marsupial.

$1 m
Annual fee paid to China for a zoo to keep a giant panda (£714,000)

175
Rhesus monkeys that escaped from Long Island Zoo in New York, USA, in 1935 – led by a monkey called Capone

1.9 MILLION
Visitors to Chester Zoo in 2017, making it the UK's second-most-visited paid-for attraction of the year

112
Animals – including hippos, elephants and baboons – kept in the first zoo, in Egypt, circa 3500 BCE

250,000+
Households signed up to San Diego Zoo Global – the largest zoological membership association

DID YOU KNOW?

The **first zoo without bars** was Tierpark Hagenbeck at Stellingen, near Hamburg, Germany. It was founded in 1907 and used deep pits and moats instead of cages to separate animals from visitors.

We're lost... Does that make us *wherewolves*?

"Grey" wolves' coats can also be – or include – black, white, brown, blond or even reddish-orange.

LARGEST WOLF ENCLOSURE

Mission: Wolf is a 26-acre (10.5-ha) naturally landscaped wolf sanctuary in the mountains of Colorado, USA. Run by the WildHeart Foundation, it focuses on sustainability – building with recycled materials and operating on solar power. The Foundation also provides support to animals in zoos and sanctuaries all over the country.

LARGEST REPTILE ZOO

Reptile Gardens in South Dakota, USA, houses more than 225 different reptilian species and subspecies.

Curator Terry Phillip (inset, with a cobra) has to handle some of the most dangerous animals in the world. Widely known for his work with snakes, he says that "although a 21-ft, 200-lb [6.4-m, 90.7-kg] python with a bad attitude will sometimes decide to get feisty... my job is really nothing glamorous. I basically clean up poo all day."

Giraffes have hair-covered horns called... a) Giraffistalks; b) Ossicones; c) Bonybeacons

173

BALLOON ZOO

At 2017's World Balloon Art Festival – held in China – things got pretty wild... Taking a deep breath, hundreds of people came together to create the **largest balloon zoo**.

ZOO

A team led by Dutch artist Guido Verhoef (see profile opposite) created a zoo with a difference on 13 Oct 2017... Every inhabitant was made out of balloons!

In all, 469,845 modelling balloons were used to create 100-plus species, including ants, sharks and dragonflies. The animals were displayed in balloon-sculpted settings and the entire installation covered an area roughly as big as two city blocks.

The epic project was organized by China's Xiamen Jimei City Development and the American Event Management Institute for the World Balloon Art Festival.

At 5.5 m (18 ft) high, the tallest animals at the zoo were the giraffes.

The balloon zoo was divided into different continents. Here, in North America, wildlife included a moose, a bald eagle and beavers.

The naturalistic surroundings, such as this colourful coral reef, demanded just as much attention as the animals!

BALLOON-BENDING PIONEERS

The origins of balloon modelling are debated. Some think the first to do it were the Aztecs. But instead of balloons, they used dried animal intestines! Eugh!

One of the contenders for the first modern "balloon-twister" was Henry Maar (USA). His act developed out of his magic show in the late 1930s.

Maar's main rival for the balloon-sculpting crown was fellow American Herman Bonnert. The story goes that he debuted the trick at a magic convention in 1939.

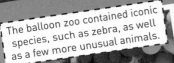
The balloon zoo contained iconic species, such as zebra, as well as a few more unusual animals.

PROFILE: GUIDO VERHOEF

Why was the balloon zoo made?
I was asked to design a large balloon installation for the World Balloon Art Festival in 2017. I love nature and wanted to give the local audience the opportunity to learn more about the beautiful and fascinating animals in the world by creating a 100% biodegradable balloon zoo.

How long did it take to complete?
After two months of preparation, we built the zoo in just 10 days. This was with the help of 200 volunteers, including local and international balloon artists.

What were the biggest challenges?
The logistics around a project of this size are extremely complicated. Planning a project with local Chinese organizers and 50 international designers who live all over the world, dealing with balloon orders, visas, flights, language and cultural differences all demand a lot of preparation.

How did you decide which animals to include?
I tried to include a mix of iconic animals and species endemic to each part of the world. The iconic animals, such as the giraffe and lion, are important to include to meet the audience's expectations, but endangered species such as the black sable antelope or the strange-looking okapi help to widen people's perspective of the animal world.

Which were the largest and smallest animals?
The whale shark in the Great Barrier Reef area was the largest and the red fire ants in South America the smallest. We tried to create all animals life-size, but we had to scale up the 40 bug species so the audience could find them!

How long have you been creating art with balloons?
I've been working with balloons for 26 years now. I started working as a performing artist when I was only 15. I learned how to make one-balloon animals and discovered the magical impact balloons have on people. It took me a few years to figure out how many different balloon sizes and shapes existed, and that you could keep adding new balloons, which creates endless possibilities.

Any tips for new balloon artists?
The only limitation is your own imagination. Dream big and work hard. The sky is not the limit any more – it's where you'll build your next project!

A walrus chills out on an iceberg in the Arctic zone.

Flamingos, koi carp and blue morpho butterflies enjoy a balloon waterfall.

Check out how to make your own balloon parrot on the next page!

Who invented the first rubber balloon? a) Michael Faraday; b) Marie Curie; c) Dee Flate

175

BALLOON ZOO

Find a video tutorial at **www.guinnessworldrecords.com/animals**

Guido Verhoef (left) was the lead artist behind the record-breaking **largest balloon zoo** on the previous page. While an entire zoo might be a bit ambitious for a beginner to attempt, here he shows you how to start with a balloon parrot. Guido recommends using your finger-widths (i.e., across the knuckles) as a measuring tool to make the model. That way, you'll always have your own ruler *to hand*!

1

Inflate two different-coloured 260-size modelling balloons (we went with red and blue), leaving about three finger-widths – roughly 5.5 cm (2 in) – uninflated. Knot them together with the two "nozzles" at the end.

HEAD

2

Twist a blue bubble of about four finger-widths long, and a slightly smaller red bubble. Now, twist the two balloons together to create the bird's head.

BODY

3

Next, create a bubble eight finger-widths long in each balloon, and twist them together to begin the body section.

4

Twist an eight-finger-width bubble in the red balloon. Bring the bubble up and wrap it around the "neck" to secure it in place. Then create a second bubble of the same length in the red balloon.

5

Bring the red bubble you just made down. With your other hand, hold the base of the main body section (as shown above).

6

To complete the parrot's body, twist all the segments together until they look like below. There should be two lengths of balloon remaining: the blue one will be much longer than the red.

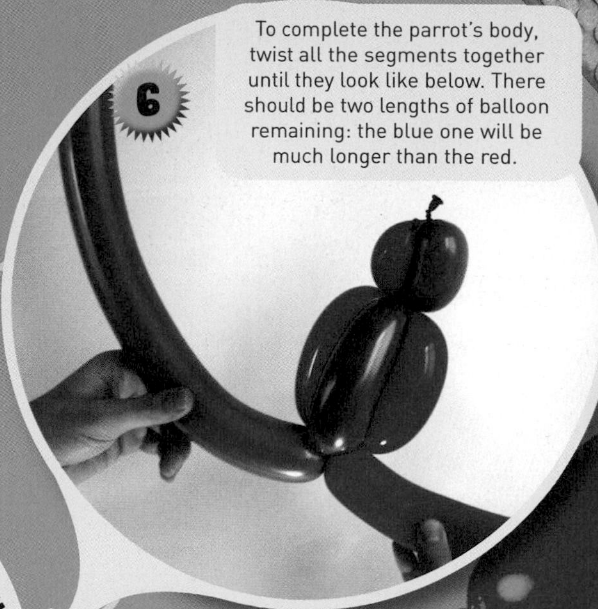

PERCH

7

For the parrot's perch, hold the end of the blue balloon and loop it over the bird's head to form a ring. Then, tie off the uninflated end at the bottom of the body.

TAIL

8

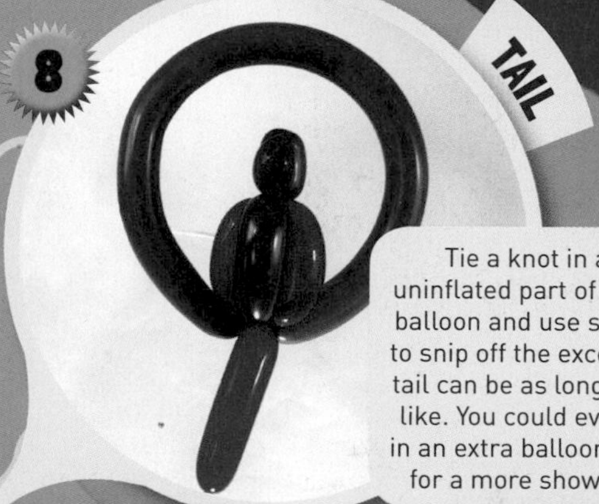

Tie a knot in any uninflated part of the red balloon and use scissors to snip off the excess; the tail can be as long as you like. You could even add in an extra balloon or two for a more showy tail!

EYES

9

A

B

C

10

You could call me Polly... but Pop-py is probably more apt!

Inflate a white 260 balloon to about six finger-widths long, and make a knot at both ends. Twist this bubble midway to form two "eyeballs" (**A**). Fold back one of the bubbles and knot the ends together (**B**); cut off the remaining uninflated part. Secure the eyes on to the head with the nozzles, then use a black marker pen/felt tip to draw on the pupils (**C**).

POLAR PLAYGROUNDS

...where bears swim in summer and skate in winter, penguins waddle in a wave machine and top predators strut their stuff in the Arctic snow.

On their very first day at the enclosure, Henry and Ganuk played in the water for 3 hr before going back to their rooms to relax.

LARGEST POLAR BEAR ENCLOSURE

Opened in 2016, the Cochrane Polar Bear Habitat in Ontario, Canada, covers an area of 5 ha (12.3 acres). With a lake (that freezes over in winter), rocks, lots of vegetation and even local wildlife, it provides as "natural" a home as possible for polar bears, the **largest bear species**. Two males – called Henry and Ganuk (right) – live in the luxury Lake Enclosure.

PROFILE: KAREN CUMMINGS, Cochrane Habitat Manager

What inspired you to create the Lake Enclosure?

Polar bears are hard animals to keep happy in human care. In the wild, they roam over vast areas, and it's difficult for a zoo to give them anything close to that. We were lucky that the lake was already on our property. We knew it froze over in winter (our climate is sub-Arctic), so we wanted to include it to mimic the bears' natural environment as much as possible. It seemed a waste not to!

What challenges did you face when creating the enclosure?

The two-year process couldn't even begin till we'd secured the funding. Then we had to find a construction company that could build 4,100 ft [1,250 m] of fencing, complete with underground "dig" barriers to prevent the bears from digging their way out. We had to clear any potential hazards (there used to be a campsite here!), move one existing road and build another all the way around the habitat. We also had to train the bears so that we could call them back to safety if we needed to.

Does other native wildlife live in and around the lake?

Yes, there's a pair of loons [water fowl], which the bears love to chase underwater. There are also otters, foxes, groundhogs, squirrels, grouse, rabbits and fish. There used to be a beaver, but when the big boys moved in, I think it decided to relocate! The foxes dart out of the bears' way at the last possible moment and the otters and loons both swim too fast for them. The dig barriers are deliberately spaced so that little animals can get in and out, but the bears stay safely enclosed.

POLK'S PENGUINS

Southern rockhoppers, with their spiky yellow-and-black crests, bound rather than waddle over craggy shores.

With around 6.3 million breeding pairs around the world, the macaroni penguin is the **most common penguin**.

A king penguin doesn't nest, but carries its single egg around on its feet, covered with a flap of skin called a "brood patch".

Gentoo penguins (see p.162 and below) are easy to spot, thanks to the white "straps" across their heads. Both parents share childcare duties.

LARGEST PENGUIN FACILITY

The Polk Penguin Conservation Center – opened in 2016 at Detroit Zoo in Michigan, USA – includes a wave machine and waterfall, as well as a 25-ft-deep (7.6-m) pool. Visitors can watch four penguin species (see above) chilling out in their winter wonderland.

An underwater viewing gallery with a huge acrylic window and two tunnels provides breathtaking views of the penguins above, around and below the water.

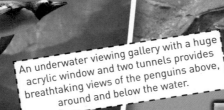

Impawssible to follow this snow trail any further: too many missing lynx...

MOST NORTHERLY ZOO

Polar Park Arctic Wildlife Centre in Troms, Norway, is located at a latitude of 68°69'N. It's home to large native predators such as Eurasian lynx (left), brown bears and wolves, as well as moose, musk ox and wolverines – the **largest weasels** (below).

Polar bears soak up warmth from the Sun with their... a) Black skin; b) Wide paws; c) Absorbent noses

AMAZING AQUARIUMS

Harnessing advanced technology and aquatic habitats inspired by nature, today's aquariums bring us closer than ever to the wonders of marine life – and beyond.

Much of SEA LIFE Brighton's Victorian Arcade is just as it was 150 years ago (see engraving below).

OLDEST AQUARIUM IN OPERATION

The UK's SEA LIFE Brighton aquarium dates from way back in 1872. Its Victorian architecture mixes with modern exhibits to show – among much else – sharks circling a tropical reef, and an Amazon rainforest complete with razor-toothed piranhas and poison-dart frogs.

PROFILE: MAX LEVISTON, SEA LIFE Brighton Manager

What's it like to manage the oldest aquarium?
It's a fascinating challenge to merge our Victorian heritage with cutting-edge exhibition technology.

How did the original aquarium come about in 1872?
As London expanded and steam trains arrived, Brighton became a popular place for wealthy people to visit. Architect and engineer Eugenius Birch designed the aquarium while he was building Brighton's West Pier.

What stories from the history of the aquarium can you reveal?
It's always been an aquarium, but it has also hosted chimpanzee tea parties, sea lions and penguins, a vintage car museum, a jazz club where The Beatles regularly performed and a dolphinarium.

How has the aquarium changed?
With improved technology, we can keep a much wider range of creatures. And human behaviour has encouraged us to focus on marine conservation and education as a major part of the visitor experience.

Do you have any favourite exhibits or species at the aquarium?
It changes every day as there's so much to see. Animal behaviours morph seasonally, too, so I never have the same favourite for long!

Sea barbels are among the first known pet fish. The Romans kept them under their beds in marble tanks.

The **largest aquarium**, China's Hengqin Ocean Kingdom, uses 48.75 million litres (12.8 million US gal) of water. The **largest fish**, whale sharks (right), can be viewed there.

The first **public aquarium** was at London Zoo, UK. The exhibit opened in May 1853 and became known simply as the "Fish House".

LARGEST OLED SCREEN

Dubai Aquarium & Underwater Zoo in The Dubai Mall, UAE, is home to an organic light-emitting diode (OLED) screen spanning 709.6 m² (7,638 sq ft). With a resolution of 1.7 billion pixels, the eye-popping display is also the **highest-resolution video wall**.

The screen is curved, like the 10-million-litre (2.6-million-US-gal) exhibit that it sits above. The huge tank contains more than 140 aquatic species, including 300 sharks and rays.

OMG!

The **largest aquarium tank**, in China, holds nine Olympic swimming pools' worth of water!

TALLEST CYLINDRICAL AQUARIUM

In 2015, the Aviapark shopping mall in Moscow, Russia, built a tank that stands a dizzying 20.3 m (66 ft 7 in) high. The aquarium holds 370,000 litres (97,743.6 US gal) of saltwater and some 2,500 fish. Divers can swim alongside the inhabitants, but must make several decompression stops on the way up from the bottom.

MOST SPECIES AT AN AQUARIUM

The Shedd Aquarium in Chicago, Illinois, USA, houses 1,500 species, including stingrays (above) and the longsnout sea horse (inset). Beyond fish, it also boasts birds, marine mammals, reptiles, amphibians and bugs – some 32,000 animals all told!

When the Shedd Aquarium first opened in Dec 1929, what vital thing was missing? a) A door; b) Water; c) Fish

INTERVIEW
JONAS LIVET

Zoo fans don't come much keener than Jonas Livet from France. He's been to 1,068 parks and sanctuaries – the **most zoos visited** – and has many more in his sights...

What was the first zoo you visited?
My first zoo was Tierpark Berlin in Germany, which I was taken to back in 1987 when I was a small child. Another early visit that made a big impression was to Tiergarten Schönbrunn in Austria [the **oldest continuously operating zoo**; see box opposite].

Got a whole otter zoos to see – no lion down on the job for me! Alpaca lunch...

The zoo was in a pretty bad state then, but now it prides itself on being a showcase for teaching and research. It's also a partner in many conservation projects, both in Austria and farther afield.

What's the farthest you've travelled to go to a zoo?
I've visited zoos in more than 50 countries around the world. Among the farthest from where I live in France are those in California, USA, South Africa and in the Far East – including China and Chinese Taipei.

Fish (and fingers?) for lunch at the Lithuanian Sea Museum in Klaipėda, where seals bask in "Sun Bay" alongside the dolphinarium.

In your opinion, which country has the best zoos?
That's a very tricky question! It depends what you're looking for – and even then, what you find there might depend on which day, or in which season you go. Dutch zoos, for example, found in both remote nature areas and in the centres of big cities, generally have a great reputation for promoting animal welfare and preservation. Czech zoos have also advanced enormously over the last two decades. Involvement in conservation is an important aspect of modern zoos, and several British zoos – including London Zoo [see pp.154–55 for an interview with ZSL's Dr Nisha Owen] are hugely committed to this.

Do you have a favourite kind of wildlife?
If I do have a weakness, it's for mammals... and hyenas are definitely among my favourites! But actually it's the way all the different species interconnect with each other that fascinates me most. Each has its own unique place in the overall scheme of things, but at the same time contributes to the whole picture. This is what's so magical about wildlife, and perhaps what drives me to keep visiting parks and sanctuaries all over the world.

Does your day job involve working with animals?
I'm lucky that I've been able to make animals the focus of my studies and all my work experience to date. When I was younger, I managed to land summer jobs and work placements as a zookeeper. At university, I trained in veterinary

JONAS RECOMMENDS...

In Switzerland, Zürich Zoo's nature-orientated enclosures include rainforests and elephant parks.

Bioparc de Doué-la-Fontaine in France designs spaces such as Rhino Valley and Leopard Canyon with specific ecosystems.

As part of its "always building" philosophy, Chester Zoo in the UK has recently opened island habitats for Malayan tapirs, Asian songbirds and Sumatran tigers (right).

Sharing a drink with an antelope in Arabia's Wildlife Centre, UAE, which boasts more than 100 species native to the Arabian Peninsula.

medicine before studying nature and wildlife management, and then conservation. This involved internships and field work that took me all over the planet.

My day job is now as a zoological consultant, which means I work with all kinds of animal parks and sanctuaries, helping to design and implement a range of projects.

Do you also go on trips to see animals in the wild?

Nothing beats seeing wildlife in its natural environment. I'm particularly keen on bird-watching. One of my most exciting trips was to California in 2013, when I not only visited some of the world's greatest zoos but also had the chance to observe wild animals in different natural settings. I saw California condors in Pinnacles National Park, for example, and lots of marine mammals in Monterey Bay.

Some people feel uneasy about zoos because they believe that animals shouldn't be confined – what are your thoughts on this?

I believe that zoos have important roles to play in society. They introduce people in a very engaging way to the huge diversity of life on Earth, and give them the opportunity and resources to find out more.

Zoos illustrate why we need to protect individual species and biodiversity as a whole – which means protecting our planet. Some zoos aren't yet doing all they can to convey these vital messages, but others are doing brilliant work and making a big difference.

Any top tips for making the most of a visit to a zoo?

It's a good idea to find out a bit about a zoo before you go – such as how it has developed over time, and what its goals and objectives are. Once you're there, take your time to observe the animals. If you can, try to talk to some of the keepers or scientists about any animals or aspects of the zoo that particularly interest you.

Which zoo will you visit next?

I think 2018 will be a busy year. I have new zoos to discover and many others I'm planning to revisit. Early in the year I'll go to Belgrade Zoo in Serbia, which first opened in 1936. Later in the spring, I'm off to Guadeloupe, where I hope to visit some zoological institutions and to see animals in the wild. Also on my list for this year are Riga Zoo in Latvia, Attica Zoological Park in Greece and the National Zoological Gardens of Sri Lanka.

With a bit of luck, I'll also visit the new Dubai Safari, which boasts all kinds of innovations including a drive-through crocodile enclosure!

What kind of reaction do you get when you visit zoos?

I try to book ahead so that I can spend time talking to staff and finding out more about the zoo and the animals. Because I've learned a great deal from my visits around the world, I often have useful experiences to share. My record for **most zoos visited** constantly reminds me how lucky I have been.

OLDEST ZOO EARNS ITS STRIPES

Tiergarten Schönbrunn in Vienna, Austria, was set up in 1752, initially as Emperor Francis I's private collection. It was opened to the public in 1779 and, still located in palace grounds to this day, is the **oldest continuously operating zoo**. Particularly proud of its achievements in breeding, successes include the birth of two giant panda cubs in 2016. Pictured here are two of the park's resident species today: zebras (left) and ring-tailed lemurs (right).

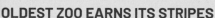

The word "zoo" is from the Greek for... a) Cage; b) Animal; c) House

THE FIONA SHOW

The first hippo calf born at Cincinnati Zoo in over 75 years, Fiona was destined for social-media stardom – even before she got her very own show on Facebook!

Young hippo Fiona is the star of "The Fiona Show" and one of the year's biggest social-media hits. She'd gained 319,638 thumbs up by 26 Apr 2018, making her the **most liked hippo on Facebook**.

Fiona was born prematurely at Cincinnati Zoo & Botanical Garden in Ohio, USA, in 2017 and became an immediate sensation. Her regular updates and video stories continue to draw new fans daily.

Fiona was underweight when she was born, so keepers bottle-fed her specially formulated milk to help her grow stronger.

Fiona was named after the female ogre in the *Shrek* movies... The similarity is apparently in the ears!

She's *hippo-notized* by all this media attention...

Fiona and her parents Henry and Bibi gaze out at their adoring public from the 70,000-US-gal (264,978-litre) pool in Hippo Cove.

ZOO-CIAL MEDIA

With 41,083 followers, Twitter's **most followed giraffe** is April from Animal Adventure Park in New York, USA. Her 15–16-month pregnancy was watched by millions.

Egyptian cobra Mia at Bronx Zoo in New York, USA, is the **most followed snake on Twitter**, with 158,750 fans. She slithered to fame after a brief escape in 2011!

*All figures correct as of 25 Apr 2018

Fiona's stomping ground – Cincinnati Zoo & Botanical Garden – is the **most liked zoo on Facebook**. It has gained 750,262 likes to date.

Hippo Cove's underwater viewing window lets Fiona's fans watch her swimming lessons with her hydrotherapist.

I've got two left feet but I'm still tons better than she is at riverdancing!

Nile hippos, also known as river horses, are vegetarians and can weigh as much as 4,000 lb (1,814 kg).
Although they spend much of their day in the water, hippos can't actually swim – they float or push off along the bottom. When they sleep in the water, their bodies automatically bob up to the surface so that they can take a breath, before sinking back down again.

13 KG

Fiona's birth weight (29 lb): about half the previous lowest weight recorded for a newborn hippo

During scanning procedures, supportive father-to-be Henry (below) would watch closely from his indoor pool and occasionally let out a reassuring bellow to his mate, Bibi.

Once keepers suspected that Bibi was to become a first-time mother, they were keen to take a peek via an ultrasound scan (inset). Easier said than done, when the mum-to-be is a 3,200-lb (1,451-kg) hippo with a penchant for belly-flopping!
To encourage her to stand still during the procedure, keepers used "positive reinforcement" – aka food bribes. As long as they kept the treats coming, Bibi would hold her position for up to 15 min, giving them plenty of time to check that all was going well.

To the trained eye, this ultrasound scan of Fiona's spine and ribs was proof positive that a star was soon to be born!

What colour is a hippo mother's milk? a) White; b) Bright pink; c) Dark blue

ANSWERS

NORTH AMERICA pp.28–29

1. Arctic fox
2. Moose
3. Caribou
4. Mountain goat
5. Narwhal
6. Harp seal
7. Brown bear
8. Fur seal
9. Musk ox
10. Snowy owl
11. Lemming
12. Black bear
13. Grey wolf
14. Lynx
15. Raccoon
16. Striped skunk
17. Great white shark
18. Willow ptarmigan
19. Coyote
20. American bison
21. Polar bear
22. Walrus
23. Wolverine
24. Puma (cougar)
25. California sea lion
26. Elk
27. American red squirrel
28. Eastern diamondback rattlesnake
29. Jaguar
30. Brown pelican
31. Seagull
32. Atlantic cod
33. Barracuda
34. Pronghorn antelope
35. California condor
36. Bottlenose dolphin

AFRICA pp.46–47

1. Fennec fox
2. Ostrich
3. Thomson's gazelle
4. Impala
5. Dromedary camel
6. Spotted hyena
7. Hornbill
8. Lion
9. Flamingo
10. Eland

11. Bottlenose dolphin
12. Nile crocodile
13. Secretary bird
14. Gorilla
15. Hammerhead shark
16. Albatross
17. Hamadryas baboon
18. Marabou stork
19. Chimpanzee
20. White rhinoceros
21. Zebra
22. Giraffe
23. Wildebeest
24. Hippopotamus
25. African elephant
26. Zebu
27. Ring-tailed lemur
28. Great white shark
29. African penguin
30. Humpback whale

AUSTRALASIA pp.114–15

1. Sperm whale
2. Whale shark
3. Southern cassowary
4. Water buffalo
5. Greater bird-of-paradise
6. Yellow-crested cockatoo
7. Red kangaroo
8. Emu
9. Green turtle
10. Koala
11. Dingo
12. Great white shark
13. Saltwater crocodile
14. Possum
15. Southern right whale
16. Bottlenose dolphin
17. Lyrebird
18. Echidna
19. Platypus
20. Fruit bat
21. Frigatebird
22. Budgerigar
23. Tasmanian devil
24. Giant devil ray
25. Jellyfish
26. Moorish idol
27. Kea
28. Swordfish
29. Kiwi
30. Kakapo
31. Octopus
32. Tuatara
33. Macaroni penguin

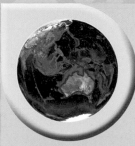

SOUTH AMERICA pp.138–39

1. Scarlet ibis
2. Bottlenose dolphin
3. Scarlet macaw
4. Golden poison-dart frog
5. Howler monkey
6. Green anaconda
7. Great white shark
8. Hummingbird
9. Sloth
10. Hyacinth macaw
11. Red-bellied piranha
12. Black pacu
13. Guanaco
14. Brown pelican
15. Capybara
16. Vicuña
17. River dolphin (boto)
18. Caiman
19. Jaguar
20. Puma (cougar)
21. South American tapir
22. Giant anteater
23. Maned wolf
24. Opossum
25. Iguana
26. Peccary
27. Rhea
28. Coypu
29. Toco toucan
30. Andean condor
31. Armadillo
32. Chilean flamingo
33. Seagull
34. Viscacha
35. Alpaca
36. Magellanic penguin

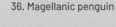

EUROPE pp.68–69

1. Bank vole
2. Fin whale
3. Harp seal
4. Harbour seal
5. Reindeer
6. Willow ptarmigan
7. Lemming
8. Moose
9. Red squirrel
10. Hare
11. Red fox
12. Atlantic cod
13. Bottlenose dolphin
14. Brown bear
15. Barn owl
16. Grey partridge
17. Roe deer
18. Grouse
19. Western capercaillie
20. Chamois
21. Iberian lynx
22. Bowhead whale
23. Osprey
24. Wild boar
25. Green frog
26. Catshark
27. White stork
28. Pine marten
29. European bison
30. Grey wolf
31. Noble deer
32. Gopher
33. Seagull
34. Mediterranean monk seal

ASIA pp.90–91

1. Western capercaillie
2. Red squirrel
3. Caspian red deer
4. Sable
5. Argali sheep
6. Grey wolf
7. Goitered gazelle
8. Snowy owl
9. Reindeer
10. Bactrian camel
11. Yak
12. Dromedary camel
13. Lemming
14. Brown bear
15. Snow leopard
16. Pika
17. Gharial
18. Harbour seal
19. Arctic fox
20. Marmot
21. Giant panda
22. Leopard
23. Asian elephant
24. Cobra
25. Green turtle
26. Lynx
27. Siberian tiger
28. Gibbon
29. Reticulated python
30. Octopus
31. Green peafowl
32. Peacock mantis shrimp
33. Hammerhead shark
34. Willow ptarmigan
35. Walrus
36. Japanese macaque
37. Whale shark
38. Flying fish
39. Sumatran rhinoceros
40. Tapanuli orangutan
41. Yellow-crested cockatoo
42. Greater bird-of-paradise
43. Tarsier

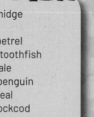

ANTARCTICA pp.162–63

1. Gentoo penguin
2. Pike icefish
3. Snow petrel
4. Southern elephant seal
5. Sei whale
6. Ross seal
7. Antarctic midge
8. Skua
9. Antarctic petrel
10. Antarctic toothfish
11. Sperm whale
12. Emperor penguin
13. Leopard seal
14. Marbled rockcod
15. Hourglass dolphin
16. Arctic tern
17. Adélie penguin
18. Blue whale
19. Weddell seal
20. Crabeater seal
21. Orca
22. Colossal squid

Below, page numbers are followed by the correct answer to the multiple-choice quiz questions. How well did you do?

10–11: b) Mermaids	86–87: c) Human souls
12–13: c) 10 million	88–89: c) On her back
14–15: a) Smell	118–19: b) Ostrich
16–17: b) Moth	120–21: a) Beer
18–19: c) Poop	122–23: c) Capybaras
20–21: a) Platypus	124–25: a) Martial arts
22–23: a) Coyote Pack	126–27: c) 200 times
24–25: b) 8	128–29: c) Australia
26–27: a) A swan	130–31: a) There's a full Moon
32–33: c) Tongues	132–33: c) Fugu
34–35: c) A flatulence	134–35: b) A grapefruit
36–37: c) Bark	136–37: a) Haul it up a tree
38–39: b) Aardvark	142–43: a) Knuckle-walking
40–41: c) Hedgehogs	144–45: b) Chi-Chi
42–43: b) African elephant	146–47: c) Black and pink
44–45: b) Cheeks	148–49: a) Rats
50–51: b) 95 million	150–51: a) Puggle
52–53: b) King penguin	152–53: b) In a nest
54–55: c) 1,500	154–55: b) Bats
56–57: c) Rosettes	156–57: a) Ankles
58–59: a) Balances sticks on its head	158–59: a) Crutching
60–61: c) 20	160–61: a) *Free Willy: Escape from Pirate's Cove* (USA, 2010)
62–63: b) Megamouth shark	166–67: a) Large jelly bean
64–65: c) Tigers	168–69: c) Its teeth
66–67: a) Baby fish	170–71: a) Nose
72–73: a) Drones	172–73: b) Ossicones
74–75: b) Roadrunner	174–75: a) Michael Faraday
76–77: c) Lungs	178–79: a) Black skin
78–79: c) Net	180–81: c) Fish
80–81: a) Dwellers	182–83: c) House
82–83: b) Dive-bomb	184–85: b) Bright pink
84–85: b) The death's-head hawk	

INDEX

CREDITS

Cover Shutterstock, Alamy; **1** Getty; **2** Shutterstock, Alamy; **3** Shutterstock; **5** Adam White, Shutterstock; **8** Shutterstock; **9** Alamy, Getty; **10** Alamy, Arthur de Bock; **11** Shutterstock, Alamy; **12** Shutterstock; **13** Shutterstock, Alamy, Getty; **14** Getty, Sylke Rohrlach; **15** Alamy; **16** FLPA, Shutterstock, Alamy; **17** Alamy, Shutterstock; **18** Shutterstock, Alamy; **19** Raymond A Mendez, Shutterstock; **20** Shutterstock, Alamy; **21** Shutterstock, Alamy; **23** Jennifer Kurt; **24** Shutterstock, Alamy; **26** Shutterstock, Alamy; **27** Alamy, SuperStock, Shutterstock; **28** Shutterstock, Alamy; **29** Shutterstock, Alamy; **30** Ardea; **31** Getty, Nature PL; **32** Alamy, Getty, Shutterstock; **33** Kiah Walker/USFWS, Alamy, Shutterstock, Getty; **34** Michael Murphy/NPWS, Shutterstock, Alamy; **35** Shutterstock, Getty; **36** Shutterstock; **37** Facebook, Shutterstock, Alamy; **38** Shutterstock; **40** Shutterstock, Alamy, Getty, Gemma Day/Country Living, Shutterstock; **42** Shutterstock, Alamy, Nature PL; **43** Alamy, Shutterstock; **44** Shutterstock; **45** Alamy, Shutterstock; **46** Shutterstock, Alamy; **47** SuperStock, Shutterstock; **48** Shutterstock; **49** Shutterstock, Alamy; **50** Alamy, Shutterstock; **51** Shutterstock, FLPA, Ardea; **52** Shutterstock; **53** Alamy, Shutterstock; **54** Shutterstock; **55** Alamy, Shutterstock; **56** Aurélien Foucault/GWR, Ge Tao/GWR; **57** Alamy; **58** Getty, iStock, Shutterstock; **59** Alamy, Shutterstock; **60** Alamy, Jiri Lochman, Shutterstock; **61** Fabio Rage, Shutterstock; **62** Alamy, Shutterstock; **63** Theodore W Pietsch/University of Washington; **64** Tadeu Oliveira/Projeto Gatos do Mato - Brasil, Shutterstock; **66** Photoshot, Shutterstock; **67** Shutterstock; **68** Shutterstock, Alamy; **69** Alamy, Shutterstock; **70** Shutterstock, Nature PL; **71** Shutterstock; **72** Shutterstock, Alamy; **74** Shutterstock; **75** Science Photo Library, Shutterstock; **76** Alamy; **77** Getty, Jonathan White, Shutterstock, Alamy; **78** NASA, Reuters; **79** Richmond Nature Park Society, Matjaz Kuntner, Getty, Enrique Peñalver Moyá, SPL, Shutterstock; **80** Colin Ralston, Getty, Alamy, Shutterstock; **81** Alamy, Shutterstock; **82** Alamy, Shutterstock; **83** Shutterstock; **84** Alamy; **85** Alamy; **86** Sarah Freeman; **87** Nick Brooks, Alamy; **88** Shutterstock; **89** Shutterstock; **90** Shutterstock; **91** Tim Laman, Shutterstock, Alamy; **92** Alamy; **93** Shutterstock; **94** Getty; **95** Shutterstock, Alamy; **96** Shutterstock; **97** Eva Koppelhus, Karkemish, Nobu Tamura, Shutterstock; **98** Shutterstock; **99** Shutterstock; **100** Shutterstock; **101** Shutterstock; **102** Shutterstock; **103** Shutterstock; **104** Shutterstock; **105** Shutterstock; **106** Shutterstock; **107** Shutterstock; **108** Shutterstock; **109** Shutterstock; **110** Alamy; **111** Alamy; **112** Alamy, Shutterstock; **113** Alamy, Shutterstock; **114** Shutterstock; **115** Shutterstock, Alamy; **116** Shutterstock; **117** Alamy, Shutterstock; **118** Shutterstock, Alamy; **119** Shutterstock, Alamy; **120** Shutterstock; **121** Shutterstock; **122** Shutterstock, Ardea, FLPA, Alamy; **123** Getty, Alamy; **124** Shutterstock, Alamy; **125** Alamy; **126** Shutterstock, Ardea, Alamy; **127** Getty, Alamy, Shutterstock; **128** Avalon, Alamy, iStock; **129** Getty, Alamy, iStock; **130** Mark O'Shea, Shutterstock, Alamy; **131** Shutterstock, Mark O'Shea; **132** Alamy, Shutterstock; **133** Alamy, Getty, Shutterstock; **134** Alamy, Shutterstock; **135** Alamy; **136** Shutterstock, Getty; **137** SuperStock, Shutterstock; **138** Shutterstock, Alamy; **139** Shutterstock; **140** Alamy; **141** Alamy, Andrea Zampatti; **142** Chase Pickering, Jane Goodall Institute, Shutterstock; **143** Shutterstock, Alamy, Michael Neugebauer, Jane Goodall Institute; **144** Jonathan Caramanus, Brent Stirton, Richard Barrett, Greg Armfield; **145** Alamy, Shutterstock, Jorge Sierra, Souvik Kundu, Brent Stirton, Richard Stonehouse; **146** Alamy, Shutterstock; **147** Shutterstock; **148** Shutterstock, BBC, Alamy, Rachel Butler/BBC; **149** David Raju, Dr Edgar Lehr, Alamy, Theo Webb/BBC, Gavin Thurston/BBC, Ifremer/A Fifis; **150** Ben Beaden, Australia Zoo; **151** Shutterstock; **152** Getty, Alamy, Shutterstock; **153** Alamy, Shutterstock; **155** Juan María Raggio, Dr KP Dinesh, Alamy; **156** Alamy, Shutterstock; **157** Alamy, Shutterstock; **158** Tibor Kércz, Carl Henry, Csaba Komaromi; **159** Olivier Colle, Daniel Trim, Katy Laveck-Foster, Andrea Zampatti, Julian Rad, Angela Bohlke; **160** Ben Beaden/Australia Zoo, Robert Irwin; **161** Russell Shakespeare/Australia Zoo, Annette Doyle/Australia Zoo; **162** Alamy, Richard E Lee, Shutterstock; **163** Shutterstock, Museum of New Zealand; **164** Getty; **165** Alamy; **166** Shutterstock, Getty, Jamie Greene; **167** Getty, Shutterstock; **168** Alex Asbury, Höskuldur Erlingsson; **169** Shutterstock, Alamy; **170** Alamy, Shutterstock; **171** Getty, Alamy, Shutterstock; **172** Getty, Alamy; **173** Getty, Kevin Scott Ramos/GWR; **174** Shutterstock; **175** Shutterstock; **176** Marc Leeflang; **179** Shutterstock, Alamy; **180** Julia Claxton, Ulrich Perrey, TopFoto; **181** Brenna Hernandez, Alamy; **183** Shutterstock, Alamy; **184** Alamy, Shutterstock; **185** Alamy, Twitter, Dave Jenike; **188** Alamy

Thanks – we couldn't have done it without you!

ACKNOWLEDGEMENTS

Claire Atkinson (Aquarium of the Pacific), Christopher Austin (Louisiana State University), Tina Campanella (ZSL), Sarah Crews (California Academy of Sciences), Stephanie Eller (Philadelphia Zoo), Victoria Fellowes (WWT), Angela Hatke (Cincinnati Zoo & Botanical Garden), Danielle Henry (Perth Zoo), Cassie Jackson (Australia Zoo), Peter Jäger (University of Senckenberg), Tom Jennings (ZSL), Mina Johnson (Seneca Park Zoo), Jonas Livet, Craig McClain (Louisiana Universities Marine Consortium), Simon Pierce (Marine Megafauna Foundation), Theodore Pietsch (University of Washington), Flo Powell, Ingo Rechenberg (Technische Universität Berlin), Dorothea Rieck (Rostock Zoo), Chance Ross (Brave Wilderness), Kelsey Ryan (Shedd Aquarium), Katsufumi Sato (University of Tokyo), Justin Schmidt (Southwest Biological Science Center), Karl Shuker, Tracey Spensley (WWF-UK), Shawn Sweeney (Jane Goodall Institute), Guido Verhoef, Angel Yanagihara (University of Hawai'i at Mānoa)

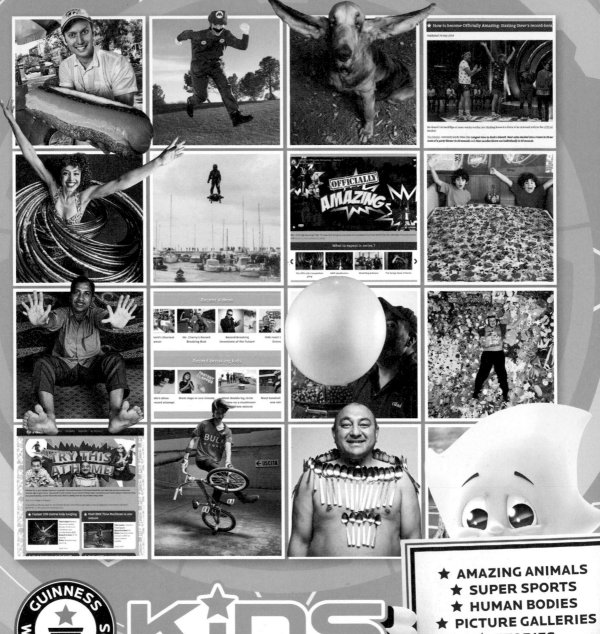